THESE THINGS WE BELIEVE

A LAYMAN'S LOOK AT THE BAPTIST FAITH AND MESSAGE

S. V. (Steve) Dedmon

International Standard Book Number 13: 978-1-60452-077-4
International Standard Book Number 10: 1-60452-077-9
Library of Congress Control Number: 2013935752

BluewaterPress LLC
52 Tuscan Way Ste 202-309
Saint Augustine FL 32092
Printed in the United States of America

http://bluewaterpress.com

This book may be purchased online at -

http://www.bluewaterpress.com/believe

DEDICATION

This is dedicated to my wife Suzanne, who has been my
greatest cheerleader

and to my daughter, Stefanie and son Seth,
in whom I am extremely proud.

PREFACE

Several years ago while attending the First Baptist Church in Jacksonville, Florida I taught a "training union" class (there is a dated church term) called "These Things We Believe." The class resulted from my experience that the membership, although constantly and consistently exposed to sound biblical preaching and teaching under the leadership of Dr. Homer G. Lindsay, Jr. and Dr. Jerry Vines, were not fully cognizant of the enumerated tenets of the faith.

Although, the first literation from the training union concept was shorter than the 18 issues addressed by the Baptist Faith and Message[1] this book extends the training union lessons and explores and expounds the Biblical principles upon which the Southern Baptist Convention considers foundational to the faith.

As I am a product of expository and alliterative preaching and teaching, initially influenced by my pastors at First Baptist, as well as Dr. John Phillips, I have embraced it as my personal teaching style. Purposefully, I have written this book in an alliterative manner, which hopefully will be easily understood as well as a medium, which will be easy to communicate. It was also written in such a manner as to keep my personal commentary to a minimum. In this way the one reading or teaching can make their own analogies as well as practical and spiritual applications. This brings me to why and to whom this has been written.

The first reason, as elementary as it may seem, is God laid it on my heart to try and convey what I have been taught and hopefully learned. In that light, as honestly as possible, I have attempted to be and hopefully have been, biblical, thus spiritually sound. My target audience is the individual who may not have given any thought to what they believe about the things of God, why they believe them, or where to find them. Whether fresh to the new believer or a refresher for those grounded in the faith, hopefully it will be educational and practical.

As to possible group training, as I did originally, this could be used as an extra curricular learning activity, like a new members or refresher type class. Finally, it could be used in a small group setting as either a series, or as topical lessons. As there are numerous topics, they could be broken down into a variety of ways to meet the spiritual needs of those to whom they would be applicable.

No matter how it is used, I pray the Lord will be glorified and the individual edified...as A Layman Looks at the Baptist Faith and Message.

---

[1] Copyright © 2000 Southern Baptist Convention. Used by permission. Text also available at http://www.sbc.net/bfm/bfm2000.asp The Southern Baptist Convention recognizes only one version of the Baptist Faith and Message at any time, and considers the earlier 1925 and 1963 renditions outdated and obsolete.

INTRODUCTION

Although there are books specifically dealing with the Baptist Faith and Message, this looks at it from purely a layman's viewpoint. The purpose of this book is to be educational, inspirational and evangelical. The text is detailed enough for a student wanting to grasp the basic spiritual context, but flexible enough for a teacher to adapt to their personal teaching style for communication of the scriptures. To this end, there is very little commentary. Each section is structured in a fashion that lends itself to be taught individually or in a series over an extended timeframe. Each chapter begins with the exact wording of the Baptist Faith and Message related to the topic and the corresponding scripture. What follows is a layman's attempt to add additional clarity, context and content.

Chapter 1, rightfully so, begins with the inerrancy of, thus importance of the scripture as it is the medium God has given man to not only reveal himself, but to disclose His story. This revelation extends not only to what He did originally but what He will do eventually. The scripture also provides the framework for our relationship to God as well as our relating to man.

In Chapter 2, God in all His fullness is discussed. God as Father, Son, and Holy Spirit are discussed as pertaining to their roles of unity in purpose and diversity in practice, as well as their divinity and distinction. Looking at God from creation, xvi - These Things We Believe

to Jesus and His revelation is the focus of this chapter. The chapter will look at God as creator, Jesus as savior and the Holy Spirit as indweller.

Chapter 3, 4, and 5 deal with man's dealing with his sin, Jesus provision of salvation, and God's sustaining grace. These chapters will draw our attention to looking internally and God's working inwardly as we face our sinful nature to ask of God what we cannot initially provide for or ultimately sustain by ourselves. The focus is therefore on identifying man's greatest need in the light of accepting God's greatest gift.

The focus of Chapters 6, 7, 8, 9, and 10 is on the ordination of the church, ordinances in the church as well as observations necessary for the church. Christ's establishment of the universality and individuality of believers in Him is discussed drawing us to focus on why He gave His life. We then see those things Christ personally did that the church/people should perpetually and willingly do as acts of worship and witness. Chapters 9, 10, and 11 specifically look at things heavenly and prophetically.

As in a previous chapter, the emphasis was to look internally, Chapters 11 through 18 concentrate on the Christian looking externally and working outwardly. The development of these chapters look at things evangelistically and educationally, all from the standpoint of a Christian's responsible to live the Gospel here on earth while looking to heaven. Chapter 13 not only outlines God's reasoning and the rewards related to one's personal finances, but a Christian's responsibility as to financing the mission and ministries of the church. Chapters 15 through 18 establish how Christians are to act in their family, community and globally.

TABLE OF CONTENTS

PREFACE	xiii
INTRODUCTION	xv
Chapter 1 - The Scriptures	1
Chapter 2 - God - The Father, Son, and Holy Spirit	5
Chapter 3 - Man and Sin	15
Chapter 4 - Salvation	19
Chapter 5 - God's Purpose of Grace	25
Chapter 6 - The Church	27
Chapter 7 - Baptism and the Lord's Supper	31
Chapter 8 - The Lord's Day	35
Chapter 9 - The Kingdom	39
Chapter 10 - Last Things	43
Chapter 11 - Evangelism and Missions	45
Chapter 12 - Education	49
Chapter 13 - Stewardship	53
Chapter 14 - Cooperation	57
Chapter 15 - The Christian and the Social Order	61
Chapter 16 - Peace and War	65
Chapter 17 - Religious Liberty	67
Chapter 18 - The Family	71
Endnotes	75
Index	79

Chapter 1 - The Scriptures

The Holy Bible was written by men divinely inspired and is God's revelation of Himself to man. It is a perfect treasure of divine instruction. It has God for its author, salvation for its end, and truth, without any mixture of error, for its matter. Therefore, all Scripture is totally true and trustworthy. It reveals the principles by which God judges us, and therefore is, and will remain to the end of the world, the true center of Christian union, and the supreme standard by which all human conduct, creeds, and religious opinions should be tried. All Scripture is a testimony to Christ, who is Himself the focus of divine revelation.

Exodus 24:4; Deuteronomy 4:1-2; 17:19; Joshua 8:34; Psalms 19:7-10; 119:11,89,105,140; Isaiah 34:16; 40:8; Jeremiah 15:16; 36:1-32; Matthew 5:17-18; 22:29; Luke 21:33; 24:44-46; John 5:39; 16:13-15; 17:17; Acts 2:16ff.; 17:11; Romans 15:4; 16:25-26; 2 Timothy 3:15-17; Hebrews 1:1-2; 4:12; 1 Peter 1:25; 2 Peter 1:19-21.

THE BIBLE IS INSPIRED BY GOD
AND WITHOUT ERROR

I. Inspiration by God (God breathed) meaning that God directed the writers all the while maintaining their personalities and peculiarities without compromising the contents/context. Many years ago, I was watching a television movie, the title of which I have long forgotten. In one scene, Paul was talking to someone and lamenting his struggles with his old and new nature, which is ultimately promulgated in Romans 7:15-20. My point is God did not necessarily dictate the scriptures to the writers but what God inspired them to write was an outgrowth of their everyday lives, thoughts and conversations.

A. Old Testament: thus saith the Lord
Exodus 4:22...thou shalt say unto Pharaoh <u>thus saith the Lord</u> (over 400 times) Isaiah 1:2...Hear, O heavens and give ear for the Lord hath spoken Jeremiah 1:4...Then the Word of the Lord came to me Jeremiah 30:2...Thus speaketh the Lord God of Israel, saying, Write all the words that I have spoken in a book.

B. New Testament: 2 Timothy 3:16...All scripture is given by inspiration of God...2 Peter 1:20-21...Knowing this first that no prophecy of the scripture is of any private interpretation. For all the prophecy came not at any time by the will of man but by holy men of God spoke as they were moved by the Holy Spirit

Writers: Kings, Prophets, Fishermen, Farmer (Gideon) Contents: 66 Books, 39 in the Old Testamnt, 27 in the New Testament, written over a period of 1,500 years. Most published/republished book translated in over 1,000 languages

II. Introduction of God John 1:1...in the beginning was the Word, and the Word was with God and the Word was God.

A. God in Creation: Genesis 1:1...in the beginning God created the heaven and earth, Psalms 19:1-6... regarding creation and His Content, Continuation, Character, Coverage, Control
1. Acts 14:17...never the less he left us not himself without a witness in that he did good and gave us rain from heaven and fruitful seasons filling

our hearts with food and gladness

2. Romans 1:20…for the invisible things of him from creation of the world are clearly seen being understood by the things that are made, even his eternal power and Godhead, so that they are without excuse

B. God in Redemption: Psalms 19:7…the law of the Lord is perfect converting the soul, John 3:16-17…For God so Loved the World, For God sent not his Son to condemn the world, but that the world through him might be saved

C. God in Revelation
    1. of himself initially, Romans 1:19-20, Psalms 19:1
    2. in His Son Ultimately, 1 Thessalonians 4:16-17… and the Lord himself shall descend…Revelation 1:1…The Revelation of Jesus Christ, which God gave unto him to show…

III. Instruction by God
  A. For our Protection:
    1. Old Testament: Psalms 119:1-176
    2. New Testament: 2 Tim. 3:16-17
      a. Doctrine: what is right
      b. Correction: what is not right
      c. Reproof: how to get right
      d. Training in righteousness: how to stay right

  B. For our Prosperity
    1. Old Testament: Joshua 1:8… this book of the law shall not depart out of thy mouth but thou shalt meditate therein day and night that thou may do according to all that is written therein for then thou shalt make thy way prosperous and then thou shalt have good success

2. New Testament: Revelation 1:3…blessed is he that readeth and they that hear the words of this prophecy, and keep those things which are written in it, for the time is at hand

IV. Inerrancy: without error

A. Practically: 2 Kings 6:6… and the Iron did swim…not to make light or jest and I do believe the ax head came to the surface, but think, but for the Titanic metal swims all the time!

B. Spiritually: if I discount what the Bible says concerning the miracle of the parting of the Red Sea should I doubt what it says about salvation? Then where do I stop, I become a debater of the word and not a doer. If I cannot believe God concerning my salvation and its miracle can I discount what it says concerning stewardship? Thus, I come up with a Bible, which is full of holes which I have created and in a crisis what if I need a part I have discarded!

V. Infallibility: will never fail, no matter the circumstances… for the…Aviator-Flight Plan, Builder-Foundation, Chef-Ingredients, Draftsman-Blueprint, Electrician-Power, Florist-Garden of Eden, Geologist-Rock of Ages, Homemaker-Heart, Inventor-Inspiration, Judge-Law of the Universe, King-Wisdom, Locksmith-Key to Life, Mason-Mortar, Navigator-Sextant, Optometrist-Light of the World, Pastor-Passion, Quarterback-Playbook, Respiratory Therapist-Breath of Life, Singer-Notes/Music, Truck Driver-Road Map, Umpire-Rules, Violinist-Symphony, Writer-Love Story, X-Ray Technician-Sight into the Unseen, Yachtsman-Compass, Zoologist-Noah's ark

Chapter 2 - God - The Father, Son, and Holy Spirit

WE BELIEVE IN THE TRINITY

Where is the Trinity found in the Bible? The word is not found in the Bible, however the Concept is found in:

Old Testament: First mention of God, Gen. 1:1, In the beginning God, in Spirit...Gen.1:2...and the Spirit of God moved upon the face of the waters. Mention of God in a plural state in an image...Gen. 1:26...and God said, Let us make man in our image, reference to Jesus the Son, Gen. 3:15...and he (Jesus) shall bruise his thy head and he (Satan) shall bruise his (Jesus) heal. One reference here to Jesus' heal is the bruising to his heal as he labored to breathe while on the cross

New Testament: The first mention of all three in one place, Matthew 3:16...Jesus when he was baptized...and he saw the Spirit of God descending like a dove...verse 17...And, lo a voice from heaven, saying, This is my Beloved Son, in whom I am well pleased. Matthew 28:19...baptizing them in the name of the Father, Son and the Holy Spirit. 1 John 5:7... For there are three that bear record in heaven, the Father, the Word *(remember John 1:14. .and the Word was made flesh and dwelt among us)* and the Holy Spirit.

I. God the Father:

God

There is one and only one living and true God. He is an intelligent, spiritual, and personal Being, the Creator, Redeemer, Preserver, and Ruler of the universe. God is infinite in holiness and all other perfections. God is all-powerful and all knowing; and His perfect knowledge extends to all things, past, present, and future, including the future decisions of His free creatures. To Him we owe the highest love, reverence, and obedience. The eternal triune God reveals Himself to us as Father, Son, and Holy Spirit, with distinct personal attributes, but without division of nature, essence, or being.

God the Father

God as Father reigns with providential care over His universe, His creatures, and the flow of the stream of human history according to the purposes of His grace. He is all-powerful, all knowing, all loving, and all wise. God is Father in truth to those who become children of God through faith in Jesus Christ. He is fatherly in His attitude toward all men.

Genesis 1:1; 2:7; Exodus 3:14; 6:2-3; 15:11ff.; 20:1ff.; Leviticus 22:2; Deuteronomy 6:4; 32:6; 1 Chronicles 29:10; Psalm 19:1-3; Isaiah 43:3,15; 64:8; Jeremiah 10:10; 17:13; Matthew 6:9ff.; 7:11; 23:9; 28:19; Mark 1:9-11; John 4:24; 5:26; 14:6-13; 17:1-8; Acts 1:7; Romans 8:14-15; 1 Corinthians 8:6; Galatians 4:6; Ephesians 4:6; Colossians 1:15; 1 Timothy 1:17; Hebrews 11:6; 12:9; 1 Peter 1:17; 1 John 5:7.

A. His Character
1. Omnipotence: Definition: God as all Powerful, God as the Almighty, Revelation 19:6...For the Lord God omnipotent reigneth, Genesis 17:1... said unto him, I am the Almighty God; walk before me and be thou perfect.
2. Omniscience: Definition: God is all knowing Psalms 147:4...He appointeth the number of the stars; he calleth them all by their names. Matthew

10:29-30…and one of them shall not fall on the ground without your Father…verse 30…but the very hairs of your head are all numbered.

3. Omnipresence: Definition: God is present at all places and all times Psalms 139:8-10…if I ascend up into heaven…make my bed in hell…dwell in the uttermost parts of the sea, thou art there.

B. His Compassion

1. Love Initiated: Old Testament: Gen. 12:1…get thee out of thy country…unto a land I will show thee; verse 2…and I will make thee a great nation, and will bless thee and make thy name great; and thou shalt be a blessing. Isaiah 49:8…Thus saith the Lord; In an acceptable time have I heard thee and in a day of salvation have I helped thee (Jesus as suffering/saving servant) New Testament: John 17:3…and this is life eternal that they might know thee, the only true God, and Jesus Christ whom thou has sent. 2 Thessalonians 1:13… because God hath from the beginning chosen you to salvation…

2. Long-suffering Demonstrated: Old Testament: Exodus 16:12…I have heard the murmurings… Exodus 17:7…they tested the Lord saying, Is the Lord among us or not? New Testament: 2 Peter 3:9…is long-suffering toward us, not willing that any should perish but that all should come to repentance.

II. Jesus the Son:

God the Son

Christ is the eternal Son of God. In His incarnation as Jesus Christ He was conceived of the Holy Spirit and born of the virgin Mary. Jesus perfectly revealed and did the will of God, taking upon Himself human nature with its demands and necessities and identifying Himself completely with mankind yet without sin. He honored the divine law by His personal obedience, and in His substitutionary death on the cross He made provision for the redemption of men from sin. He was raised from the dead with a glorified body and appeared to His disciples as the person who was with them before His crucifixion. He ascended into heaven and is now exalted at the right hand of God where He is the One Mediator, fully God, fully man, in whose Person is effected the reconciliation between God and man. He will return in power and glory to judge the world and to consummate His redemptive mission. He now dwells in all believers as the living and ever present Lord.

Genesis 18:1ff.; Psalms 2:7ff.; 110:1ff.; Isaiah 7:14; 53; Matthew 1:18-23; 3:17; 8:29; 11:27; 14:33; 16:16,27; 17:5; 27; 28:1-6,19; Mark 1:1; 3:11; Luke 1:35; 4:41; 22:70; 24:46; John 1:1-18,29; 10:30,38; 11:25-27; 12:44-50; 14:7-11; 16:15-16,28; 17:1-5, 21-22; 20:1-20,28; Acts 1:9; 2:22-24; 7:55-56; 9:4-5,20; Romans 1:3-4; 3:23-26; 5:6-21; 8:1-3,34; 10:4; 1 Corinthians 1:30; 2:2; 8:6; 15:1-8,24-28; 2 Corinthians 5:19-21; 8:9; Galatians 4:4-5; Ephesians 1:20; 3:11; 4:7-10; Philippians 2:5-11; Colossians 1:13-22; 2:9; 1 Thessalonians 4:14-18; 1 Timothy 2:5-6; 3:16; Titus 2:13-14; Hebrews 1:1-3; 4:14-15; 7:14-28; 9:12-15,24-28; 12:2; 13:8; 1 Peter 2:21-25; 3:22; 1 John 1:7-9; 3:2; 4:14-15; 5:9; 2 John 7-9; Revelation 1:13-16; 5:9-14; 12:10-11; 13:8; 19:16.

A. His Claim
      1. His Equality with God: Old Testament: Isaiah 9:6...
      and his name shall be called...The Mighty God, The
      Everlasting Father. New Testament: John 14:9-11...
      He that hath seen me hath seen the Father...vrs 11...
      Believe me that I am in the Father and the Father in
      me.
      2. His Deity as God: Old Testament: Psalms 110:1...
      the Lord said unto my Lord sit thou at my right
      hand...New Testament: John 8:58, Jesus said...
      verily, I say unto you, Before Abraham was, I am
      ...Colossians 2:9-10...For in him dwelleth all the
      fullness of the Godhead bodily...verse 10...who is
      the head of all principality and power.
      3. His Humanity: Old Testament: Isaiah 9:6...for
      unto us a child is born, unto us a son is given.
      New Testament: Matthew 2:1, 9... when Jesus was
      born...verse 9...where the young child was.
      Matthew 4:1-11.. the temptation of Jesus. Jesus
      ate, wept, thirst, and John 19:33 died...

B. His Call
      1. A Son for God: Luke 1:32...He shall be great and
      shall be called the Son of the Highest.
      2. A Savior for Man Luke 2:11...in the city of David
      a Savior who is Christ the Lord. Matthew 1:21...
      and thou shalt call his name JESUS, for he shall
      save the people from their sin. Luke 19:10...for
      the Son of man is come to seek and to save that
      which was lost.

C. His Conception
His Conception: Old Testament: Isaiah 7:13-14...Therefore
the Lord himself shall give you a sign; Behold the virgin
shall conceive and bear a son and shall call his name
Immanuel (God with Us) Although this was to Ahaz it
was a prophetic statement to the House of David
(see verse 13)

New Testament: Matthew 1:18...before they came together, she (Mary) was found with child of the Holy Spirit

Note: for years we have been arguing the concept of immaculate conception with the world. Now, even Hollywood appears to have embraced the concept. One of the movies in the Star Wars collection, revolves around Anakin Skywalker (ultimately becoming Darth Vadar) as a young boy. When his mother is questioned by a Jedi knight about his father, she says he has none and she just conceived. This could be looked as the world validating (not that what God has ever done, or will do, in any way needs human validation) everything we have ever defended concerning the virgin birth. Of course the context is not the same, but the content is, as the world will eventually validate ALL the things of God!

D. The Consequences
    1. Practically
        a. Mary's Amazement: Luke 1:27, 34...how shall this be seeing I know no man... verse... 27...Gabriel...sent from God...to a virgin espoused to a man whose name was Joseph. Note here the Catholic belief and the thought of Mary as favored... Luke 1:28 and the angel came in unto her and said thou art highly favored, the Lord is with thee: blessed art thou among women. Luke 1:42...Blessed art thou among women
        b. Joseph's Predicament: Matthew 1:19...then Joseph her husband being a just man and not willing to make her a public example... Joseph's options: Divorce or Death
        c. Joseph's Acknowledgment: Matthew 1:20-25...thought on these things... verse 24... Then Joseph...did as the angel of the Lord had bidden him and took unto him his wife

   2. Spiritually
      a. Generally: The bloodline is traced through the Father. So, the original sin of Adam would ccurse through his veins if tracing his bloodline in this regard; however:
   3. Genealogy:
      a. Father: His Royalty - Luke 2:4: And Joseph...(because he was of the house and lineage of David)
      b. Mother: His Purity/Humanity - Matthew 1:16...and Jacob begat Joseph the husband of Mary "<u>of whom was born</u>" Jesus. Then, not begat by the natural but was born of the supernatural. Thus, as related to Jesus and to him only, the inheritance of a sin nature of Adam does not flow from the bloodline of the natural father. His sinlessness flowed from his supernatural father. This is the same one experiences in salvation. We have a natural birth but it takes us "being born of the spirit" a supernatural birth to become children of God. Look at John 3 and Nicodemus - begat naturally, born again supernaturally!

III. God the Holy Spirit

God the Holy Spirit

The Holy Spirit is the Spirit of God, fully divine. He inspired holy men of old to write the Scriptures. Through illumination He enables men to understand truth. He exalts Christ. He convicts men of sin, of righteousness, and of judgment. He calls men to the Saviour, and effects regeneration. At the moment of regeneration He baptizes every believer into the Body of Christ. He cultivates Christian character, comforts believers, and bestows the spiritual gifts by which they serve God through His church. He seals the believer unto the day of final redemption. His presence in the Christian is the guarantee that

God will bring the believer into the fullness of the stature of Christ. He enlightens and empowers the believer and the church in worship, evangelism, and service.

Genesis 1:2; Judges 14:6; Job 26:13; Psalms 51:11; 139:7ff.; Isaiah 61:1-3; Joel 2:28-32; Matthew 1:18; 3:16; 4:1; 12:28-32; 28:19; Mark 1:10,12; Luke 1:35; 4:1,18-19; 11:13; 12:12; 24:49; John 4:24; 14:16-17,26; 15:26; 16:7-14; Acts 1:8; 2:1-4,38; 4:31; 5:3; 6:3; 7:55; 8:17,39; 10:44; 13:2; 15:28; 16:6; 19:1-6; Romans 8:9-11,14-16,26-27; 1 Corinthians 2:10-14; 3:16; 12:3-11,13; Galatians 4:6; Ephesians 1:13-14; 4:30; 5:18; 1 Thessalonians 5:19; 1 Timothy 3:16; 4:1; 2 Timothy 1:14; 3:16; Hebrews 9:8,14; 2 Peter 1:21; 1 John 4:13; 5:6-7; Revelation 1:10; 22:17.

A. as Comforter

John 14:6...and I will pray the Father and he shall give you another Comforter that he may abide with you forever. John 16:7...Nevertheless I tell you the truth: It is expedient for you that I go away; for if I go not away, the Comforter will not come... Romans 8:16...The Spirit himself beareth witness with our spirit that we are the children of God.

B. as Counselor

I John 2:20...But ye have an unction from the Holy One, and ye know all things.

Positive leading: Acts 8:29...and the Spirit said unto Philip, Go near, and join thyself to this chariot.

Negative leading: Acts 16:7...After they were come to Mysia they attempted to go into Bithynia; but the Spirit allowed them not.

WE BELIEVE IN THE PERSON OF THE HOLY SPIRIT

What does one think of when you think of a person?

I. His Personality
   A. Intellect: 1 Corinthians 2:10-11...But God hath revealed them to us by his Spirit; for the Spirit searcheth all things. Yea the deep things of God, verse. 11...for what man knoweth the things of man which is in him? Even so the things of God knoweth no man, but the Spirit of God (thus the Spirit must have intelligence to know the things of God). Ephesians 4:30...And grieve not the Holy Spirit...
   B. Dialect:
   New Testament: Acts 8:26...but the Spirit himself maketh intercession for us with groanings, which cannot be uttered (*note the case to make for those espousing a prayer language could come from this verse).
   Old Testament: Ezekiel 3:12...Then the Spirit lifted me up and I heard behind me a voice of a great rushing, saying, Blessed be the glory of the Lord from his place. 1 Timothy 4:1...Now the Spirit speaketh expressly that...

II. His Presence
   A. Indwelling:
   New Testament: 1 Corinthians 6:19...What? Know ye not that your body is the temple of the Holy Spirit who is in you...John 14:17 Jesus said...Even the Spirit of Truth... but ye know him; for he dwelleth with you and shall be in you.
   Old Testament: Daniel 4:8-9... in whom (Daniel) is the spirit of the gods (remember Nebuchadnezzar was polytheistic at this point, thus gods).
      1. At Salvation: Ephesians 1:13...in whom also after ye believed, ye were sealed with that Holy Spirit of Promise (Here some denominations make the claim for a 2nd Baptism, speaking in tongues, et cetera)

B. Enabling:

    1. As a Witness: Acts 2:4,8…And they were all filled with the Holy Spirit and began to speak with other tongues…verse. 8…and how hear we every man in our own tongue, wherein we were born (note these versus are used along with those in I Corinthians, above, to reinforce those who advocate the modern day gift of speaking in tongues).

    2. In our Ways and our Walk: Galatians 5:22-23…for the fruit of the Spirit is …verse 25…if we live in the Spirit, let us also walk in the Spirit. 1 Corinthians 12:7,28…manifestation of the Spirit is given to every man to profit, verse 28, apostles…prophets, teachers, healings, helps, governments

    Note: while we are here: the difference between an Indwelling and a Filling. There is always an indwelling of the Spirit of those who are saved as that is <u>God's promise</u>, but, the constant Filling is <u>our prerogative</u> …see Ephesians 5:18…be not drunk with wine but be filled with the Spirit

Chapter 3 - Man and Sin

Man is the special creation of God, made in His own image. He created them male and female as the crowning work of His creation. The gift of gender is thus part of the goodness of God's creation. In the beginning man was innocent of sin and was endowed by his Creator with freedom of choice. By his free choice man sinned against God and brought sin into the human race. Through the temptation of Satan man transgressed the command of God, and fell from his original innocence whereby his posterity inherit a nature and an environment inclined toward sin. Therefore, as soon as they are capable of moral action, they become transgressors and are under condemnation. Only the grace of God can bring man into His holy fellowship and enable man to fulfill the creative purpose of God. The sacredness of human personality is evident in that God created man in His own image, and in that Christ died for man; therefore, every person of every race possesses full dignity and is worthy of respect and Christian love.

Genesis 1:26-30; 2:5,7,18-22; 3; 9:6; Psalms 1; 8:3-6; 32:1-5; 51:5; Isaiah 6:5; Jeremiah 17:5; Matthew 16:26; Acts 17:26-31; Romans 1:19-32; 3:10-18,23; 5:6,12,19; 6:6; 7:14-25; 8:14-18,29; 1 Corinthians 1:21-31; 15:19,21-22; Ephesians 2:1-22; Colossians 1:21-22; 3:9-11.

I. Sin's Origination:

    A. Heavenly

            1. Satan's Indignation: Isaiah 14:13-17 (spoken of previously and the five I wills)

    B. Earthly

            1. Man's Creation: Genesis 1:26...Let us make man in our own image,* after our likeness vrs 2:7... And the Lord God formed man...and breathed into his nostrils the breath of life...and man became a living soul

               formed - body

               breath of life - spirit

               living soul - soul *So man has a triune nature, in the image of a Triune God

                  a. Fellowship: Genesis 3:8...And they heard the voice of the Lord God walking in the garden in the cool of the day...

                  b. Followship: Genesis 2:17...But of the tree of the knowledge of good and evil, thou shalt not eat

            2. Man's Temptation: Genesis 3:6...saw that it was good for food - appealing,...pleasant to the eyes - attractive,...desired to be wise - all knowing...Genesis 3:5...For God doth know that in the day ye eat thereof, then your eyes shall be opened, and ye shall be as God, knowing good and evil.

            3. Man's Capitulation: Genesis 3:6...she took of the fruit thereof, and did eat and gave also unto her husband with her; and he did eat.

II. Sin's Definition:

    A. Sins of Commission: those that I do Psalms 51:4...Against thee, thee only have I sinned and done this evil in thy sight. Romans 7:19...the evil which I would not, that I do

B. Sins of Omission: those thing I should or do not do. Romans 7:19...For the good that I would do I do not do. James 4:17...Therefore to him to knoweth to do good and doeth it not to him it is sin

C. Sins of Presumption: Presuming to think God does not know or care about what I do, Psalms 19:13...Keep thy servant also from presumptuous sins. Let them not have dominion over me. Numbers 15:30...but the soul that doest anything presumptuously

III. Sin's Destruction:

A. Universally: Romans 5:12...Wherefore as by one man sin entered into the world and death by sin and so death passed upon all men, verse 18...by the offense of one judgment came upon all men to condemnation

B. Personally: Romans 3:23...For all have sinned and come short of the Glory of God, Romans 7:18...For I know that in me dwelleth no good
   1. Depravity: involves all the attributes of man
      a. Intellectually: Romans 1:28...as they did not like to retain God in their knowledge (root) verse 29-31 (fruit)
      b. Consciously: 1 Timothy 4:2...having their conscience seared
      c. Willfully: John 20:25...Thomas...except I see,...put,. .thrust,...I will not believe.
      d. Wholly: Ephesians 4:17-18...walk not as other Gentiles, in the vanity of their minds, verse 18...Having their understanding darkened, being alienated from the life of God.
      e. Totally: Old Testament: Psalms 119:133... Order my steps...and let not any iniquity have dominion over me. 1 John 1:18...If we say we have not sin, we deceive ourselves

IV. Sin's Originator - Satan

A. his Formation
> 1. his Beauty: Ezekiel 28:12-15...full of wisdom, and perfect in beauty
> 2. his Duty: Ezekiel 28:13...the workmanship of thy tabrets (timbles) and of thy pipes (flutes) was prepared in thee in the day that thou wast created - Heavenly Choir Director

B. his Fall: Isaiah 14:12-17...How art thou fallen from heaven. O Lucifer. Son of the morning! verse 13-14...the five (5) "I wills" of the Satan...New Testament: Luke 10:18...I (Jesus) beheld Satan as lightning fall from heaven

C. his Focus
> 1. To Deceive the Lost: Ephesians 2:2...In which times past ye walked according to the course of this world, according to the prince of the power of the air, the spirit that now worketh in the sons of disobedience...Revelations 20:10...and that devil that deceived them
> 2. To Defeat the Saved: 1 Chronicles 21:1...and Satan stood up against Israel, and enticed David to number Israel. Revelation 12:10...for the accuser of our brethren is cast down. Job 1:6-12... verse 11 and he (Job) will curse thee (God) to thy face.

D. his Finality: Revelation 20:10...the devil...was cast into the lake of fire...and shall be tormented forever and ever

Chapter 4 - Salvation

Salvation involves the redemption of the whole man, and is offered freely to all who accept Jesus Christ as Lord and Savior, who by His own blood obtained eternal redemption for the believer. In its broadest sense salvation includes regeneration, justification, sanctification, and glorification. There is no salvation apart from personal faith in Jesus Christ as Lord.

A. Regeneration, or the new birth, is a work of God's grace whereby believers become new creatures in Christ Jesus. It is a change of heart wrought by the Holy Spirit through conviction of sin, to which the sinner responds in repentance toward God and faith in the Lord Jesus Christ. Repentance and faith are inseparable experiences of grace.

Repentance is a genuine turning from sin toward God. Faith is the acceptance of Jesus Christ and commitment of the entire personality to Him as Lord and Savior.

B. Justification is God's gracious and full acquittal upon principles of His righteousness of all sinners who repent and believe in Christ. Justification brings the believer unto a relationship of peace and favor with God.

C. Sanctification is the experience, beginning in regeneration, by which the believer is set apart to God's purposes, and is enabled to *progress toward moral and spiritual maturity through the presence and power of the Holy Spirit dwelling in him. Growth in grace should continue throughout the regenerate person's life.*

    D. Glorification is the culmination of salvation and is the final blessed and abiding state of the redeemed.

    Genesis 3:15; Exodus 3:14-17; 6:2-8; Matthew 1:21; 4:17; 16:21-26; 27:22-28:6; Luke 1:68-69; 2:28-32; John 1:11-14,29; 3:3-21,36; 5:24; 10:9,28-29; 15:1-16; 17:17; Acts 2:21; 4:12; 15:11; 16:30-31; 17:30-31; 20:32; Romans 1:16-18; 2:4; 3:23-25; 4:3ff.; 5:8-10; 6:1-23; 8:1-18,29-39; 10:9-10,13; 13:11-14; 1 Corinthians 1:18,30; 6:19-20; 15:10; 2 Corinthians 5:17-20; Galatians 2:20; 3:13; 5:22-25; 6:15; Ephesians 1:7; 2:8-22; 4:11-16; Philippians 2:12-13; Colossians 1:9-22; 3:1ff.; 1 Thessalonians 5:23-24; 2 Timothy 1:12; Titus 2:11-14; Hebrews 2:1-3; 5:8-9; 9:24-28; 11:1-12:8,14; James 2:14-26; 1 Peter 1:2-23; 1 John 1:6-2:11; Revelation 3:20; 21:1-22:5.

I. Sin's Substitution: Old Testament

    A. Sorrowful Inception: Genesis 3:8-11, ...and Adam and his wife hid themselves from the presence of the Lord God, verse. 10...I heard thy voice...and I was afraid, verse. 11...Hast thou eaten of the tree whereof I commanded thee that thou shouldest not eat?

    B. Holy Provision: Genesis 3:21...the Lord God made coats of shin and clothed them (what does this verse not say) the death of the animals - thus the coats are a result of the sacrifice. Genesis 22:8...My son God will provide himself a lamb for a brunt offering (Look at this verse in Context - see verse. 13) then/or "provide himself" a lamb - interesting!

    C. Jewish/Cultural Tradition: Exodus 12:5, 7, 13-14, ...your lamb shall be without blemish, verse. 7...And they shall take of the blood and strike it on the two side posts and on the upper door post of the houses, verse 13...and when I see the blood, I will pass over, verse 14...And this day shall be unto you as a memorial; and ye shall keep it a feast to the Lord throughout your generations

II. Son's Crucifixion, New Testament to Provide:

A. Propitiation: ask forgiveness, offer of apology, ask for a pardon (courtroom analogy) Romans 3:25...whom God hath set forth to be a propitiation, 1 John 2:2...And he is the propitiation for our sins (John speaking) 1 John 4:10... sent his Son to be the propitiation for our sins

B. Redemption: to pay a price (courtroom analogy it is the restitution phase) being redeemed at the slave market of sin. Note also the book of Ruth as the Biblical application of Kinsman redeemer
Old Testament: Psalms 19:14...Let the words of my mouth ...and meditation of my heart be acceptable in thy sight O, Lord and redeemer
New Testament: Romans 3:25...Being justified...by his grace through the redemption that is in Jesus. Ephesians 1:7...In whom we have redemption through his blood even the forgiveness of sins. Also Colossians 1:14...just about the same exact wording as Paul writes again - authenticity of the scripture
   1. Willingness: John 10:17-18...I lay down my life, verse. 18...no man taketh it from me
   2. Sinlessness: John 1:29...Behold the Lamb of God who taketh away the sin of the world. John 8: 46...Which of you convicteth me of sin? 1 Peter 1:19...But with the precious blood of Christ, as of a lamb without blemish and without spot

C. Substitution: Matthew 20:28...and to give his life a ransom for many. (Mark 10:45 same wording) 2 Corinthians 5:21...For he hath made him, who knew no sin, to be sin for us that we may be the righteousness of God. 1 Peter 3:18...For Christ also hath once suffered for sins, the just for the unjust that he might bring us to God

D. Regeneration: John 3:3...except a man be born again, John 3:5...except a man be born of water and of the Spirit, he cannot see the kingdom of God. 2 Corinthians 5:17...if any man be in Christ he is a new creation...Romans 6:6... Knowing this that our old man is crucified with him...

E. Glorification: Romans 8:18...the sufferings of this present time are not worthy to be compared to the glory which shall be revealed in us. 1 John 3:2...and it doth not yet appear what we shall be, (but) we know that, when he shall appear, **we shall be like him, for we shall see him as he is**

JUSTIFICATION BY FAITH

I. Faith's justification

A. Individually: Romans 3:28...Therefore we conclude that a man is justified by faith apart from the deeds of the law

B. Universally: Romans 3:29-30...Is he the God of the Jews only...not also of the Gentiles — seeing it is one God, who shall justify the circumcision by faith and the uncircumcision through faith

II. Faith's definition: Hebrews 11:1: For faith is the substance of things hoped for the evidence of things not seen

A. Appropriation: Romans 10:17...So then, faith cometh by hearing, and hearing by the word of God. Psalms 119:41: Let thy mercies come also unto me, O Lord, even thy salvation according to thy word

B. Application: Romans 4:5: But to him that worketh not, but believeth on him that justifieth the ungodly (me) his faith is counted for righteousness. Romans 1:17: For in it (the Gospel) is the righteousness (righteousness is the fraternal twin of justification) of God revealed from faith to faith; as it is written the just (or justified) shall live (initially, daily, and eternally) by faith. Hebrews 11:6... But without faith it is impossible to please him; for he that cometh to God must believe that he is and that he is a rewarder of them that diligently seek him

II. Faith and its role in:

A. Repentance: Ephesians 2:8...For by grace are ye saved through faith... 1 Peter 1:9...Receiving the end of your faith, even the salvation of your souls.

B. Assurance: 1 John 5:4...For whatever is born of God overcometh the world: and this is the victory that overcometh the world, even our faith.

Chapter 5 - God's Purpose of Grace

Election is the gracious purpose of God, according to which He regenerates, justifies, sanctifies, and glorifies sinners. It is consistent with the free agency of man, and comprehends all the means in connection with the end. It is the glorious display of God's sovereign goodness, and is infinitely wise, holy, and unchangeable. It excludes boasting and promotes humility.

All true believers endure to the end. Those whom God has accepted in Christ, and sanctified by His Spirit, will never fall away from the state of grace, but shall persevere to the end. Believers may fall into sin through neglect and temptation, whereby they grieve the Spirit, impair their graces and comforts, and bring reproach on the cause of Christ and temporal judgments on themselves; yet they shall be kept by the power of God through faith unto salvation.

Genesis 12:1-3; Exodus 19:5-8; 1 Samuel 8:4-7,19-22; Isaiah 5:1-7; Jeremiah 31:31ff.; Matthew 16:18-19; 21:28-45; 24:22,31; 25:34; Luke 1:68-79; 2:29-32; 19:41-44; 24:44-48; John 1:12-14; 3:16; 5:24; 6:44-45,65; 10:27-29; 15:16; 17:6,12,17-18; Acts 20:32; Romans 5:9-10; 8:28-39; 10:12-15; 11:5-7,26-36; 1 Corinthians 1:1-2; 15:24-28; Ephesians 1:4-23; 2:1-10; 3:1-11; Colossians 1:12-14; 2 Thessalonians 2:13-14; 2 Timothy 1:12; 2:10,19; Hebrews 11:39–12:2; James 1:12; 1 Peter 1:2-5,13; 2:4-10; 1 John 1:7-9; 2:19; 3:2.

I. Grace's definition: God's unmerited favor

    A. Unexplainable: Old Testament Economy: Psalm 8:4-6...
What is man, that thou art mindful of him?, verse 5...
hast crowned him with glory and honor, verse. 6...thou
madest him to have dominion over the works of thy
hands, thou hast put all things under his feet
New Testament Economy: Romans 8:16, 17...the Spirit
himself beareth witness...that we are children of God,
verse. 17...And if children, then heirs - heirs of God, and
joint heirs with Christ. Romans 5:1...Therefore being
justified by faith we have peace with God through our
Lord Jesus Christ

    B. Unmerited: Ephesians 2:8: for by grace are ye saved
through faith...it is the gift of God, Romans 3:26...To
declare I say at this time his (Jesus') righteousness that
he (Jesus) might be just and the justifier of him (me) who
believeth in Jesus

    C. Unearnable: Romans 4:4-5...Now to him that worketh is
the reward not reckoned of grace but of debt, verse.
5...but to him that worketh not but believeth on him
that justifieth the ungodly. Galatians 2:16...man is not
justified by the works of the law, for by the works of the
law shall no man be justified (Note: the context is that
of Judaism but it is not distorting the scripture to make it
applicable to me.) Ephesians 2:9...Not of works...

    D. Unending: Romans 8:35, 37-39...Who shall separate us
from the love of Christ? Shall tribulation or distress, or
persecution, or famine or nakedness, or peril or sword?...
verse 37... Nay, in all these things we are more than
conquerors through him that loved us. Verse 38...For I
am persuaded, that neither death, nor life, nor angels,
nor principalities, nor powers, nor things present, nor
things to come,...verse 39...Nor height, nor depth, nor any
other creature, shall be able to separate us from the love
of God, which in in Christ Jesus our Lord

Chapter 6 - The Church

A New Testament church of the Lord Jesus Christ is an autonomous local congregation of baptized believers, associated by covenant in the faith and fellowship of the gospel; observing the two ordinances of Christ, governed by His laws, exercising the gifts, rights, and privileges invested in them by His Word, and seeking to extend the gospel to the ends of the earth. Each congregation operates under the Lordship of Christ through democratic processes. In such a congregation, each member is responsible and accountable to Christ as Lord. Its scriptural officers are pastors and deacons. While both men and women are gifted for service in the church, the office of pastor is limited to men as qualified by Scripture.

The New Testament speaks also of the church as the Body of Christ, which includes all of the redeemed of all the ages, believers from every tribe, and tongue, and people, and nation.

Matthew 16:15-19; 18:15-20; Acts 2:41-42,47; 5:11-14; 6:3-6; 13:1-3; 14:23,27; 15:1-30; 16:5; 20:28; Romans 1:7; 1 Corinthians 1:2; 3:16; 5:4-5; 7:17; 9:13-14; 12; Ephesians 1:22-23; 2:19-22; 3:8-11,21; 5:22-32; Philippians 1:1; Colossians 1:18; 1 Timothy 2:9-14; 3:1-15; 4:14; Hebrews 11:39-40; 1 Peter 5:1-4; Revelation 2-3; 21:2-3.

I. The Church in the Public

A. Jesus Initially Mentions **the Church**...Matthew 16:18...
That thou art Peter, and upon this rock I will build my
church, and the gates of hell shall not prevail against it.
Matthew 18:17...And if he shall neglect to hear them, tell
it unto the **church**; but if he neglect to hear the **church**...
Acts 2:41-42, 44, 46-47...Then they that gladly received
his word were baptized...verse 42...and they continued
steadfastly in the apostles' doctrine and fellowship...
verse 44...And all that believed were together...verse
46...And they, continuing daily with one accord in the
temple...verse 47..Praising God, and having favor with all
the people, And the Lord added to the **church** daily such
as should be saved

II. The Church in the Person

A. Royalty: 1 Peter 2:5, 9, 10: Ye also as living stones are
built up a spiritual house, and holy priesthood...verse
9...But ye are a chosen generation, a royal priesthood, an
holy nation a peculiar people (a people of his own), verse.
10...but are now the people of God

B. Equality: Romans 8:17: And if children then heirs-heirs of
God, and joint heirs with Christ. Galatians 3:26, 29: For
ye are the sons of God by faith...verse. 29 and if ye be
Christ's then are ye Abraham's seed and heirs according
to the promise

C. Accessibility: Hebrews 4:16: Let us, therefore, come
boldly unto the throne of grace... Matthew 27:51...And
behold, the veil of the temple was torn in two from the
top to the bottom... Hebrews 10:19...having therefore,
brethren boldness to enter into the holiest by the blood
of Jesus

D. Accountability:

    1. Personal:

        a. Offering: 1 Peter 2:5...to offer up spiritual sacrifices acceptable to God by Jesus Christ

        b. Assembling: Hebrews 10:25...Not forsaking the assembling of ourselves together as the manner of some is but...Psalms 122:1: I was glad when they said unto me, Let us go into the house of the Lord

        c. Exhorting: Hebrews 10:25...exhorting one another so much the more as ye see the day approaching

    2. Evangelical: Hebrews 10:23:...Let us hold fast the profession of our faith without wavering

III. The Church and Its Positions

A. Its Pastoral Ministry

    1. Man: 1 Timothy 3:1... If a man...

        a. Desire: 1 Timothy 3:1... desire of the office...

        b. Discipline: 1 Timothy 3:2-7... blameless, monogamous, righteous...

    2. Mandate: 2 Timothy 4:1... preach the word...

    3. Methodology: 2 Timothy 4:1... be diligent in season, out of season... reprove, rebuke, exhort with all long-suffering and doctrine

B. Its Deacon Ministry

    1. The Need: Acts 6:1... daily administration

        a. Tasks within the Church: Acts 6:1-2... serving the women and the brethren

        b. Tasks outside the Church: Acts 6:8... full of faith

    2. Their Nature: 1 Timothy 3:8-13... their speech, their spending, their standing

Chapter 7 - Baptism and the Lord's Supper

Christian baptism is the immersion of a believer in water in the name of the Father, the Son, and the Holy Spirit. It is an act of obedience symbolizing the believer's faith in a crucified, buried, and risen Savior, the believer's death to sin, the burial of the old life, and the resurrection to walk in newness of life in Christ Jesus. It is a testimony to his faith in the final resurrection of the dead. Being a church ordinance, it is prerequisite to the privileges of church membership and to the Lord's Supper.

The Lord's Supper is a symbolic act of obedience whereby members of the church, through partaking of the bread and the fruit of the vine, memorialize the death of the Redeemer and anticipate His second coming.

Matthew 3:13-17; 26:26-30; 28:19-20; Mark 1:9-11; 14:22-26; Luke 3:21-22; 22:19-20; John 3:23; Acts 2:41-42; 8:35-39; 16:30-33; 20:7; Romans 6:3-5; 1 Corinthians 10:16,21; 11:23-29; Colossians 2:12.

Ordinances of the Church
Obedience by the Individual

BAPTISM:

I. Memorialized by Jesus:

    A. Baptism's Importance: Matthew 3:13-15: Then cometh Jesus from Galilee to the Jordan unto John to be baptized by him (this was a walk of 120 miles) verse 15...for thus it becometh us to fulfill all righteous

B. Baptism's Identification: Romans 6:1-5: verse. 5, For if we have been planted together in the likeness of his death, we shall be also raised in the likeness of his resurrection. Note we say buried with Christ in the likeness of his death raised in the glorious likeness of his resurrection

II. Method:

A. Immersion: the Greek word baptizo means to be immersed. Additionally, it was the customary practice of the Jews of a proselyte to Judaism to immerse totally (submersion) Matthew 3:16: And Jesus when he was baptized went up straightway out of the water.

As a Note: methods of baptisms recognized by other denominations:
Effusion - to pour
Aspersion - to sprinkle

III. Mandate:

A. For: In the words of the Great Commission, ...baptizing them in the name of the Father, and of the Son and of the Holy Spirit. Acts 8:36...What doth hinder me to be baptized? verse 37...And Philip said, if thou believest with all thine heart thou mayest. Acts 8:12...But when they believed Philip preaching the things concerning the kingdom of God and the name of Jesus Christ they were baptized, both men and women

B. Against: You can use all the verses above and separate the believing from the baptism. John 3:16...whosoever believeth in him, verse 18...He that believeth on him is not condemned. Acts 2:21...and it shall come to pass that whosoever shall call on the name of the Lord shall be saved. Luke 23:43...Today shalt thou be with me in paradise

THE LORD'S SUPPER:

I. Words of Interpretation:
Eucharist: a celebration of the Lord's Supper
Communion: an action or situation involving sharing

A. Sacrament/Ordinance: synonyms literally, antonyms practically Sacrament: something presented to the senses, which has the power by divine institution not only of signifying, but also of efficiently conveying grace (Roman Catholic Council of Trent)
Ordinance: that which Jesus himself by his doing established for the church

B. Symbolism or Sacrament: We believe the elements, the bread and the cup are symbolic of the body and blood of Christ, not that it is His literal body or that there is a dispensation of grace in its partaking.

II. Jesus Instituted: Luke 22:19, 20...he took bread and gave thanks and broke it...saying This is my body which is given for you this do in remembrance of me, verse 20...Likewise also the cup. This cup is the New Testament in my blood.

III. We Imitate:

A. Examination: 1 Corinthians 11:28...But let a man examine himself, and so let him eat of that bread and drink of that cup

B. Unification: 1 Corinthians 10:16...The cup of blessing... the bread which he broke is it not the communion of the body of Christ, verse 17...For we being many are one body for we are all partakers of that one bread

C. Anticipation: 1 Corinthians 11:26... ye do show the Lord's death till he come

Chapter 8 - The Lord's Day

The first day of the week is the Lord's Day. It is a Christian institution for regular observance. It commemorates the resurrection of Christ from the dead and should include exercises of worship and spiritual devotion, both public and private. Activities on the Lord's Day should be commensurate with the Christian's conscience under the Lordship of Jesus Christ.

Exodus 20:8-11; Matthew 12:1-12; 28:1ff.; Mark 2:27-28; 16:1-7; Luke 24:1-3,33-36; John 4:21-24; 20:1,19-28; Acts 20:7; Romans 14:5-10; 1 Corinthians 16:1-2; Colossians 2:16; 3:16; Revelation 1:10.

Old Testament

I. God: Establishes the Priorities of Worship
  The Sabbath is:
  A. Holy...Exodus 20:8...Remember the Sabbath day,
     to keep it holy. Proverbs 96:9...worship the Lord in the beauty of holiness. Exodus 20:11...wherefore the Lord blessed the Sabbath day and hallowed it.
  B. Healthy...Exodus 20:9...Six days shalt thou labor
     and do all thy work...verse 10...But the seventh day...in it thou shalt not do any work...20:11...in six days the Lord made the heaven and earth, the sea, and all that is in them is and rested the seventh day.

C. His...Exodus 20:10...But the seventh day <u>is the Sabbath of the Lord thy God</u>...Psalms 95:6...Oh, come, let us worship and bow down; let us kneel before the Lord our maker.

New Testament

II. Satan: Entices the Perversion of Worship

A. Attempts to Change the Objective of Worship...Matthew 4:8...again the devil...and showed him all the kingdoms of the world, and the glory of them, verse 9, And saith unto him, <u>All these things I will give thee</u>...as opposed to...Matthew 6:33...But seek ye first the kingdom of God and his righteousness and all these things shall be added unto you.

B. Attempts to Change the Object of Worship...Matthew 4:9... <u>if thou wilt fall down and worship me</u>...as opposed to... Matthew 4:10...Then saith Jesus unto him, Begone, Satan; for it is written, Thou shalt worship the Lord, thy God, and him only shalt thou serve.

III. Religion: Expands the Practice of Worship

A. Defined by Ritual...Matthew 12:1-2...Jesus went on the Sabbath day through the grainfields; and his disciples were hungry and began to pluck the ears of grain and to eat...verse 2...But when the Pharisees saw it, they said unto him, Behold they disciples do that which is not lawful to do upon the Sabbath day. Matthew 12:9... And they asked him, saying, Is it lawful to heal on the Sabbath days... that they might accuse him.

IV. Jesus: Embodies the Person of Worship

A. Defined by Relationship...Matthew 12:8...For the Son of man is Lord even of the Sabbath day. Matthew 16:15-16, 18...But who say ye that I am? Verse 16...And Simon

Peter answered and said, Thou art the Christ the son of the living God...verse 18...and upon this rock I will build my church, and the gates of hell shall not prevail against it. Acts 2:38...Then Peter said unto them, Repent, and be baptized, every one of you, in the name of Jesus Christ for the remission of sins...verse 42...and they continued steadfastly in the apostles' doctrine and fellowship and in breaking of bread, and in prayers...verse 46...and they, continuing daily with one accord in the temple.

Chapter 9 - The Kingdom

The Kingdom of God includes both His general sovereignty over the universe and His particular kingship over men who willfully acknowledge Him as King. Particularly the Kingdom is the realm of salvation into which men enter by trustful, childlike commitment to Jesus Christ. Christians ought to pray and to labor that the Kingdom may come and God's will be done on earth. The full consummation of the Kingdom awaits the return of Jesus Christ and the end of this age.

Genesis 1:1; Isaiah 9:6-7; Jeremiah 23:5-6; Matthew 3:2; 4:8-10,23; 12:25-28; 13:1-52; 25:31-46; 26:29; Mark 1:14-15; 9:1; Luke 4:43; 8:1; 9:2; 12:31-32; 17:20-21; 23:42; John 3:3; 18:36; Acts 1:6-7; 17:22-31; Romans 5:17; 8:19; 1 Corinthians 15:24-28; Colossians 1:13; Hebrews 11:10,16; 12:28; 1 Peter 2:4-10; 4:13; Revelation 1:6,9; 5:10; 11:15; 21-22.

I. The God of the Kingdom Ministry...Genesis 1:1...In the beginning God created the heaven and the earth. In the end...Revelation 21:1-2...And I saw a new heaven and new earth, for the first heaven and the first earth were passed away...verse 2...And 1 John saw the holy city, new Jerusalem, coming down from God out of heaven...

II. The Gospel of the Kingdom Ministry and its...Matthew 13:1-58

    A. Profession...Matthew 13:24-25...*The kingdom of heaven* is likened unto a man which sowed good seed in his field...verse 25...but...his enemy came and sowed tares among the wheat. Note co-existing but not co-mingling. **Parting**... Matthew 13:30...Gather ye together first the tares, and bind them in bundles to burn them: but gather the wheat into my barn.

    B. Planting...Matthew 13:31...*The kingdom of heaven* is like a grain of mustard which a man took and sowed in his field...**Potential**...verse 32...Which, indeed, is the least of all seeds...**Protection**...but when it is grown it is the greatest among herbs, and becometh a tree, so that the birds of the air come and lodge in the branches thereof.

    C. Pollution...Matthew 13:33...*The kingdom of heaven* is like leaven...**Potency**...which a woman took , and hid in three measure of meal, till the whole was leavened.
        Leaven of the false doctrines of the...
        1. Pharisees...Legalism
        2. Sadducees...Liberalism and Skepticism
        3. Herodians...Materialism

    D. Preciousness...Matthew 13:44...*The kingdom of heaven* is like treasure hidden in a field (which when a man hath found, he hideth, and for joy of it goeth and selleth all that he hath, and buyeth that field. John 3:16...For God so loveth the world that he gaveth his only begotten son...verse 17...For God sent not his Son into the world to condemn the world, but that the world through him might be saved - contrast - God's ultimate sacrifice verses man's unforgivable sin. Matthew 16:26...For what profit a man to gain the whole world and lose his own soul

    E. Pricelessness...Matthew 13:45...Again, *the kingdom of heaven* is like a merchant man, seeking fine pearls...verse

46...Who, when he had found one pearl of great price, went and sold all that he had, and bought it...Ephesians 5:25... even as Christ also loved the church and gave himself for it. Ephesians 2:20...And built upon the foundation of the apostles and prophets Jesus Christ himself being the chief corner stone.

F. Parting...Matthew 13:47...Again, *the kingdom of heaven* is like a net that was cast into the sea, and gathered of every kind. Matthew 13:49...at the end of the age, the angels shall come forth and separate/sever the wicked from among the righteous/just.

G. Participation...Matthew 13:52...*the kingdom of heaven* is like a man that is a householder, who bringeth forth out of his treasure things new and old.
   1. Insight
   2. Instruction
   3. Inspiration

III. The Glory of the Kingdom Ministry and its

   A. Preaching... Mark 1:14-15... Jesus came into Galilee preaching the gospel of the kingdom of God And saying, The time is fulfilled, and the kingdom of God is at hand: repent ye, and believe the gospel. Luke 4:43-44...And he said unto them, I must preach the kingdom of God to other cities also; for therefore am I sent...verse 44...And he preached in the synagogues of Galilee.

   B. Power...Matthew 6:13...For thine is the kingdom, and the power, and the glory, forever. Amen. John 3:3...Jesus answered and said unto him, Verily, verily, I say into thee, Except a man be born again he cannot see the kingdom of God.

Chapter 10 - Last Things

God, in His own time and in His own way, will bring the world to its appropriate end. According to His promise, Jesus Christ will return personally and visibly in glory to the earth; the dead will be raised; and Christ will judge all men in righteousness. The unrighteous will be consigned to Hell, the place of everlasting punishment. The righteous in their resurrected and glorified bodies will receive their reward and will dwell forever in Heaven with the Lord.

Isaiah 2:4; 11:9; Matthew 16:27; 18:8-9; 19:28; 24:27,30,36,44; 25:31-46; 26:64; Mark 8:38; 9:43-48; Luke 12:40,48; 16:19-26; 17:22-37; 21:27-28; John 14:1-3; Acts 1:11; 17:31; Romans 14:10; 1 Corinthians 4:5; 15:24-28,35-58; 2 Corinthians 5:10; Philippians 3:20-21; Colossians 1:5; 3:4; 1 Thessalonians 4:14-18; 5:1ff.; 2 Thessalonians 1:7ff.; 2; 1 Timothy 6:14; 2 Timothy 4:1,8; Titus 2:13; Hebrews 9:27-28; James 5:8; 2 Peter 3:7ff.; 1 John 2:28; 3:2; Jude 14; Revelation 1:18; 3:11; 20:1-22:13.

I. Expectantly: Titus 2:13...Looking for that blessed hope and the glorious appearing of the great God and our Savior, Jesus Christ. 2 Timothy 4:8...but unto all them also that love his appearing. The context is that we shall receive crowns of righteousness at his appearing

II. Personally: John 14:3...I will come again and receive you unto myself that where I am ye maybe also. Luke 21:27...they shall see the Son of man coming in a cloud. 1 Thessalonians 4:16-17...For the Lord himself shall descend...

III. Audibly: 1 Corinthians 15:52...at the last trump, for the trumpet shall sound. 1 Thessalonians 4:16-17...with a shout, with the voice of the archangel and with the trump of God

IV. Visually: Luke 21:27...And then they shall see the Son of man coming in a cloud. Acts 1:9-11...received him out of their sight, verse 11...shall so come in like manner as ye have seen him go into heaven

V. Eternally: 1 Corinthians 52-57...verse 54...this mortal shall put on immortality 1 Thessalonians 4:17...and so shall we ever be with the Lord

Chapter 11 - Evangelism and Missions

It is the duty and privilege of every follower of Christ and of every church of the Lord Jesus Christ to endeavor to make disciples of all nations. The new birth of man s spirit by God's Holy Spirit means the birth of love for others. Missionary effort on the part of all rests thus upon a spiritual necessity of the regenerate life, and is expressly and repeatedly commanded in the teachings of Christ. The Lord Jesus Christ has commanded the preaching of the gospel to all nations. It is the duty of every child of God to seek constantly to win the lost to Christ by verbal witness undergirded by a Christian lifestyle, and by other methods in harmony with the gospel of Christ.

Genesis 12:1-3; Exodus 19:5-6; Isaiah 6:1-8; Matthew 9:37-38; 10:5-15; 13:18-30, 37-43; 16:19; 22:9-10; 24:14; 28:18-20; Luke 10:1-18; 24:46-53; John 14:11-12; 15:7-8,16; 17:15; 20:21; Acts 1:8; 2; 8:26-40; 10:42-48; 13:2-3; Romans 10:13-15; Ephesians 3:1-11; 1 Thessalonians 1:8; 2 Timothy 4:5, Hebrews 2:1-3; 11:39-12:2; 1 Peter 2:4-10; Revelation 22:17.

I. The Great Commission

    A. Our Commander: Matthew 28:18…And Jesus came and spoke unto them saying, All power/authority is given unto me in heaven and in earth. John 20:21…as my Father hath sent me, even so send I you

B. Our Command: Matthew 28:19...Go ye therefore, Mark 16:15...Go ye into...Now we know the context is... <u>as I go</u> through the routines of my life.
1. <u>Community/City</u>: Acts 1:8...ye shall be witnesses unto me both in Jerusalem
2. <u>Country</u>: Acts 1:8...in all Judaea
3. <u>Continent</u>: Acts 1:8...in all Samaria
4. <u>Corner</u> (every): Acts 1:8...unto the uttermost part of the earth

C. Our Communiqué: Matthew 28:19-20...teach all nations... teaching them to observe all things whatsoever I have commanded you
1. Sin: Romans 3:10...As it is written, There is none righteous, no, not one. Romans 3:23...for all have sinned and come short of the glory of God
2. Salvation: Luke 19:10...For the Son of man is come to seek and to save that which was lost. John 1:29...Behold the Lamb of God who taketh away the sin of the world. 1 Peter 3:18...For Christ also hath once suffered for sins, the just for the unjust that he might bring us to God... Old Testament, Isaiah 53:7...All have gone astray...each to his own way, and the Lord hath laid on him the iniquity of us all.
3. Separation: 2 Corinthians 6:17...Wherefore come out from among them and be ye separate saith the Lord. Ephesians 5:1...Be ye, therefore followers of God as dear children. Ephesians 4: 24-29: ...put on the new man, verse 25...putting away, verse 27...Neither give place to the devil, verse 29 steal no more, verse 29...let no corrupt communication proceed out of your mouth...

D. Our Comfort: Matthew 28:20...and, lo, I am with you always even unto the end of the world/age. Acts 1:8...But ye shall receive power after the Holy Spirit is come upon you. Acts 4:29, 31: Grant unto thy servants that with all boldness they may speak thy word, verse 31...the place was shaken, they were all filled with the Holy Spirit, and they spoke the word of God with boldness

II. The Challenge:

It is our responsibility to make sure the Great Commission does not become the Great Omission.

A. Availability:
Old Testament Context:
Isaiah 6:8...Also I heard the voice of the Lord, saying, Whom shall I send, and who will go for us? Then said I, Here am I; send me.
New Testament Context:
Matthew 9:37-38...The harvest truly is plenteous, but he laborers are few. Pray ye, therefore the Lord of the harvest, that he will send forth laborers into this harvest, Luke 10:2... The harvest truly is great, but the laborers are few... 1 Thessalonians 1:8...For from you sounded out the word of the Lord...in every place your faith toward God is spread abroad...

B. Accountability:
Old Testament Context:
Ezekiel 3:18...When I say unto the wicked, Thou shalt surely die; and thou givest him not warning, nor speakest to warn the wicked from his wicked way to save his life, the same wicked man shall die in the iniquity; but this blood will I require at thine hand...Yet if thou warn the wicked, and he turns not from his wickedness nor from his wicked way, he shall die in his iniquity; but thou has delivered thy soul.
New Testament Context:
Romans 1:16...For I am not ashamed of the gospel of Christ, for it is the power of God unto salvation to everyone that believeth; to the Jew first, and also to the Greek, Hebrews 2:1...we ought to give the more earnest

heed to the things which we have heard, lest at any time we should let them slip...

We must remember we Will Never Be Soul Winners until We are Soul **Seers**!!!

Chapter 12 - Education

Christianity is the faith of enlightenment and intelligence. In Jesus Christ, abide all the treasures of wisdom and knowledge. All sound learning is, therefore, a part of our Christian heritage. The new birth opens all human faculties and creates a thirst for knowledge. Moreover, the cause of education in the Kingdom of Christ is co-ordinate with the causes of missions and general benevolence, and should receive along with these the liberal support of the churches. An adequate system of Christian education is necessary to a complete spiritual program for Christ's people.

In Christian education, there should be a proper balance between academic freedom and academic responsibility. Freedom in any orderly relationship of human life is always limited and never absolute. The freedom of a teacher in a Christian school, college, or seminary is limited by the pre-eminence of Jesus Christ, by the authoritative nature of the Scriptures, and by the distinct purpose for which the school exists.

Deuteronomy 4:1,5,9,14; 6:1-10; 31:12-13; Nehemiah 8:1-8; Job 28:28; Psalms 19:7ff.; 119:11; Proverbs 3:13ff.; 4:1-10; 8:1-7,11; 15:14; Ecclesiastes 7:19; Matthew 5:2; 7:24ff.; 28:19-20; Luke 2:40; 1 Corinthians 1:18-31; Ephesians 4:11-16; Philippians 4:8; Colossians 2:3,8-9; 1 Timothy 1:3-7; 2 Timothy 2:15; 3:14-17; Hebrews 5:12-6:3; James 1:5; 3:17.

I. Proclaiming the Word

    A. Priest's Presentation
          1. Openly...Nehemiah 8:2...And Ezra the priest brought the law before the congregation... men and women...and all that could hear with understanding...verse 5...and Ezra opened the book in the sight of all the people
          2. Distinctly...Nehemiah 2:8...So they read in the book in the law of God distinctly...verse 3...And he read therein...verse 6...And Ezra blessed the Lord, the great God.

    B. Christ's Affirmation
          1. His Manner...Luke 2:46...found him in the temple, sitting in the midst...verse 47...all that heard him were astonished at his understanding and answers. Matthew 4:23...And Jesus went about all Galilee, teaching in their synagogues. Matthew 5:2...and he opened his mouth and taught them saying,. Mark 2:38...Let us go into the next towns that I may preach there also: for therefore came I forth
          2. His Message...Luke 8:1...shewing the glad tidings of the kingdom of God. Luke 19:10...For the Son of man is come to seek and to save that which was lost. John 1:29...Behold the Lamb of God, which taketh away the sin of the world. Matthew 4:23... and preaching the gospel of the kingdom.

II. Receiving the Word

    A. People's Reception...Nehemiah 8:3...and the ears of all the people were attentive unto the book of the law.

    B. People's Reverence...Nehemiah 8:5...all the people stood... verse 6...answered, Amen, Amen...lifting up their hands and they bowed their heads.

III. Comprehending the Word... Job 28:28...Behold, the fear of the Lord, that is wisdom; and to depart from evil is understanding. James 1:5...If any of you lack wisdom, let him ask of God, that giveth to all men liberally and upbraideth not and it shall be given him. James 3:17...But the wisdom that is from above is first pure, then peaceable, gently, and easy to be intreated...

IV. Obeying the Word...Matthew 7:24...whosoever heareath these sayings of mine, and doeth them. 2 Timothy 3:14-16...But thou continue in the things which thou hast learned... verse 15...And that from a child thou has known the holy scriptures. James 1:22...But be ye doers of the word, and not hearers only -
We would rather **Debate** the Word of God than **Do** the Word of God.

V. Preserving the Word...Philippians 2:16...Holding forth the word of life. Colossians 3:16...Let the word of Christ dwell in you richly, in all wisdom teaching and admonishing one another...I Timothy 5:17...Let the elders that rule well be counted worthy of double honor, especially they who labor in the word and doctrine. 2 Timothy 4:2...Preach the word; be diligent in season, out of season; reprove, rebuke, exhort with all long-suffering and doctrine.

Chapter 13 - Stewardship

God is the source of all blessings, temporal and spiritual; all that we have and are we owe to Him. Christians have a spiritual debtorship to the whole world, a holy trusteeship in the gospel, and a binding stewardship in their possessions. They are therefore under obligation to serve Him with their time, talents, and material possessions; and should recognize all these as entrusted to them to use for the glory of God and for helping others. According to the Scriptures, Christians should contribute of their means cheerfully, regularly, systematically, proportionately, and liberally for the advancement of the Redeemer's cause on earth.

Genesis 14:20; Leviticus 27:30-32; Deuteronomy 8:18; Malachi 3:8-12; Matthew 6:1-4,19-21; 19:21; 23:23; 25:14-29; Luke 12:16-21,42; 16:1-13; Acts 2:44-47; 5:1-11; 17:24-25; 20:35; Romans 6:6-22; 12:1-2; 1 Corinthians 4:1-2; 6:19-20; 12; 16:1-4; 2 Corinthians 8-9; 12:15; Philippians 4:10-19; 1 Peter 1:18-19.

I. The Tithe Established

    A. An Act of Worship - Genesis 14:20...And blessed be the most high God, who hath delivered thin enemies into thy hand. And he gave him tithes of all.

        1. Did not Have To

        2. Did not Hate To

Looking at Possessions not Persons...Genesis 14:21...And the king of Sodom said unto Abram, Give me the persons, and take the goods to thyself. There are various implications and ramifications associated with this verse. For example, the King of Sodom (and Satan) always look at people to <u>pervert them</u> while God looks at the person <u>to provide for them</u>.

B. An Act of Witness - Genesis 14:22...And Abram said to the king of Sodom, I have lifted up mine hand unto the Lord, the most high God, the possessor of heaven and earth.

C. An Act of Wisdom - Genesis 15:1-5...After these things the word of the Lord came unto Abram in a vision, saying, Fear not, Abram: I am thy shield, and thy exceedingly great reward...Look now toward heaven, and count the stars. if thou be able to number them; and he said unto him, So shall thy seed be.

II. The Tithe Explained - Leviticus 27:31-32

A. Its Author...Leviticus 27:30...all the tithe...is holy unto the Lord

B. Its Owner...Leviticus 27:30...all the tithe...is the Lord's

C. Its Common Denominator... Leviticus 27:32...the tenth
Thus, there are no big or little givers in God's economy, we are all equal.

III. The Tithe Expounded - Malachi 3:7-12

A. God asks if We will <u>Return</u>...verse 7
B. God asks if We will <u>Rob</u>...verse 8
C. God says We will <u>Receive</u>...verse 10
D. God says He will <u>Rebuke</u>...verse 11

IV. The Tithe Expanded

    A. Beyond the Financial...Luke 11:41-42...But rather give alms of such things as ye have...For ye tithe mint and rue and all manner of herbs, and pass over justice and the love of God; these ought ye to have done.

    B. Beyond the Nominal...Mark 12:41-44...Jesus sat (verse.41)... Jesus saw (beheld, verse 41), Jesus says (saith)...This poor widow hath cast more in than all they who have cast into the treasury
        1. Giving Abundantly...verse 44...For all they did cast in of their abundance...**verses**
        2. Giving Sacrificially...verse 44...but she of her want did cast in <u>all</u> that she had, even <u>all</u> her living

Jesus looking at the tithe...
Condoned the tithe...Luke 11:42...For woe unto you Pharisees! For ye tithe mint and rue and all manner of herbs, and pass over justice and the love of God; <u>these</u> (the tithe) <u>ought ye to have done</u>, and not to leave the other undone. Thus, ...did not Condemn the tithe
Additionally and to be taken seriously...

        3. Giving Purposefully, Necessarily, Not Grudgingly, but Cheerfully... 2 Corinthians 9:7... Every man according as he purposeth in the heart, sot let him give, not grudgingly, or of necessity: for God loveth a cheerful giver.

However: Giving Cheerfully is no excuse for Giving Obediently...Malachi 3:10...Bring ye all the tithes into the storehouse...saith the Lord of hosts.

Chapter 14- Cooperation

Christ's people should, as occasion requires, organize such associations and conventions as may best secure cooperation for the great objects of the Kingdom of God. Such organizations have no authority over one another or over the churches. They are voluntary and advisory bodies designed to elicit, combine, and direct the energies of our people in the most effective manner. Members of New Testament churches should cooperate with one another in carrying forward the missionary, educational, and benevolent ministries for the extension of Christ's Kingdom. Christian unity in the New Testament sense is spiritual harmony and voluntary cooperation for common ends by various groups of Christ's people. Cooperation is desirable between the various Christian denominations, when the end to be attained is itself justified, and when such cooperation involves no violation of conscience or compromise of loyalty to Christ and His Word as revealed in the New Testament.

Exodus 17:12; 18:17ff.; Judges 7-21; Ezra 1:3-4; 2:68-69; 5:14-15; Nehemiah 4; 8:1-5; Matthew 10:5-15; 20:1-16; 22:1-10; 28:19-20; Mark 2:3; Luke 10:1ff.; Acts 1:13-14; 2:1ff.; 4:31-37; 13:2-3; 15:1-35; 1 Corinthians 1:10-17; 3:5-15; 12; 2 Corinthians 8-9; Galatians 1:6-10; Ephesians 4:1-16; Philippians 1:15-18.

I. The Practicality of Christian Ministry

    A. Doing the Mundane - Exodus 17:11-12...when Moses held up his hand that Israel prevailed: and when he let down his hand, Amalek prevailed, verse 12...But Moses' hands were heavy...and Aaron and Hur stayed up his hands. the one on the one , and the other on the other side. Exodus 13:19...And Moses took the bones of Joseph with him: for he had straitly sworn the children of Israel...saying, God will surely visit you, Joshua 6:3...And ye shall compass the city, all ye men of war, and go round about the city once. Thus shalt thou do six days. Acts 8:29, 35, 38...Then the Spirit said unto Philip, Go near, and join thyself to this chariot, verse 35...Then Philip opened his mouth... and preached unto him Jesus, verse 38...and he baptized him.---**So Philip's one...see below**

    B. Resulting in the Magnificent - Exodus 17:13...And Joshua vanquished Amalek and his people with the edge of the sword. Joshua 24:32...And the bones of Joseph, which the children of Israel brought up out of Egypt, buried they in Shechem, in a parcel of ground which Jacob bought of the sons of Hamor...and it became the inheritance of the children of Joseph. Joshua 6:20...and the people shouted with a great shout, that the wall fell down flat so that the people went up into the city, every man straight before him, and they took the city. Acts 2:14, 41...But Peter, standing up with the eleven, lifted up his voice, verse 41...and the same day there were added unto them about three thousand souls.---**verses Paul's three thousand... see above**

II. The Diversity of Christian Ministry - Romans 12:4, 5, 6, ...
For as we have many member in one body, and all members have not the same office, verse 5...So we being many, are one body in Christ, and every one members one of another, verse 6...Having then gifts differing according to the grace that is given to us. 1 Corinthians 3:6...I have planted, Apollos watered; but God gave the increase

III. The Unity of Christian Ministry - 1 Corinthians 1:10...
Now I beseech you, brethren by the name of our Lord Jesus Christ, that ye all speak the same thing, and that here be no divisions among you, but that ye be perfectly joined together in the same mind, Philippians 2:5...Let this mind be in you, which was also in Christ Jesus. Philippians 3:15...Let us therefore, as many as be perfect, be thus minded: and if in anything ye be otherwise minded, God shall reveal even this unto you.

IV. The Complexity of Christian Ministry - 1 Corinthians 1:12-13...
Now this I say, that every one of you saith, I am of Paul; and I of Apollos; and I of Cephas; and I of Christ, verse 13...Is Christ divided? Galatians 2:11-12, 14...But when Peter was come to Antioch, I withstood him, verse 12...For before that certain came from James, he did eat with the Gentiles; but when they were come, he withdrew and separated himself, fearing them which were of the circumcision. Verse 14...If thou, being a Jew, livest after the manner of Gentiles, and not as do the Jews, why compellest thou the Gentiles to live as do the Jews?

Chapter 15 - The Christian and the Social Order

All Christians are under obligation to seek to make the will of Christ supreme in our own lives and in human society. Means and methods used for the improvement of society and the establishment of righteousness among men can be truly and permanently helpful only when they are rooted in the regeneration of the individual by the saving grace of God in Jesus Christ. In the spirit of Christ, Christians should oppose racism, every form of greed, selfishness, and vice, and all forms of sexual immorality, including adultery, homosexuality, and pornography. We should work to provide for the orphaned, the needy, the abused, the aged, the helpless, and the sick. We should speak on behalf of the unborn and contend for the sanctity of all human life from conception to natural death. Every Christian should seek to bring industry, government, and society as a whole under the sway of the principles of righteousness, truth, and brotherly love. In order to promote these ends Christians should be ready to work with all men of good will in any good cause, always being careful to act in the spirit of love without compromising their loyalty to Christ and His truth.

Exodus 20:3-17; Leviticus 6:2-5; Deuteronomy 10:12; 27:17; Psalm 101:5; Micah 6:8; Zechariah 8:16; Matthew 5:13-16,43-48; 22:36-40; 25:35; Mark 1:29-34; 2:3ff.; 10:21; Luke 4:18-21; 10:27-37; 20:25; John 15:12; 17:15; Romans 12–14; 1Corinthians 5:9-10; 6:1-7; 7:20-24; 10:23-11:1; Galatians 3:26-28; Ephesians 6:5-9; Colossians 3:12-17; 1 Thessalonians 3:12; Philemon; James 1:27; 2:8.

I. Speaking Truthfully - Zechariah 8:16...These are the things that ye shall do; speak ye every man the truth to his neighbor...

II. Acting Honorably

    A. A Christian's Attitude - Luke 10:33-37...But a certain Samaritan...when he saw him, he had compassion on him, verse 36...Which now of these...was neighbor unto him that fell among the thieves, verse 37...And he said, He that shewed mercy on him. Then said Jesus unto him, Go, and do thou likewise.

    B. A Christian's Actions - Zechariah 8:16...execute the judgment of truth.
        1. As salt - Matthew 5:13...ye are the salt of the earth... to preserve, to protect, to purify
        2. As light - Matthew 5:14...ye are the light of the world..to shine, to show, to serve, verse 16...that they may see your good works and glorify your Father which is in heaven.

    C. A Christian's Affections - Matthew 22:37...Thou shalt love the Lord thy God will all thy heart, and with all thy soul and all thy mind...AND, Matthew 22:39... and the second is like unto it, thou shalt love they neighbor as thyself.

III. Walking Justly and Humbly - Micah 6:8...what does the Lord require of thee, but to do justly, and to love mercy and to walk humbly with thy God?

IV. Giving Generously - Luke 6:38...Give, and it shall be given unto you; good measure, pressed down, and shaken together, and running over, shall men give unto your bosom. For with the same measure that ye mete withal it shall be measured to you again.

V. Responding Submissively

A. To Those Maintaining Authority - Matthew 22:17...
[I]s it lawful to give tribute unto Caesar, or not?....verse
21...[R]ender unto therefore, unto Caesar the things
which are Caesar's; and to God, the things that are God's.

B. To Those Advocating Hostility - Matthew 18:15...Moreover,
if thy brother shall trespass against thee, go and tell
him his fault between thee and him alone; if he shall
hear thee, thou hast gained thy brother (note also
verses 16 and 17). Luke 6:27-28...But I say unto you that
hear, Love your enemies, do good to then who hate
you,...Bless then that curse you and pray for then who
despitefully use you.

Chapter 16 - Peace and War

It is the duty of Christians to seek peace with all men on principles of righteousness. In accordance with the spirit and teachings of Christ, they should do all in their power to put an end to war.

The true remedy for the war spirit is the gospel of our Lord. The supreme need of the world is the acceptance of His teachings in all the affairs of men and nations, and the practical application of His law of love. Christian people throughout the world should pray for the reign of the Prince of Peace.

Isaiah 2:4; Matthew 5:9,38-48; 6:33; 26:52; Luke 22:36,38; Romans 12:18-19; 13:1-7; 14:19; Hebrews 12:14; James 4:1-2.

I. Prince of Peace

A. Christ and His Sovereignty Over Nations - Isaiah 2:4...And he shall judge among the nations, and shall rebuke many people: and they shall beat their swords into plowshares, and their spears into pruning hooks: nation shall not lift up sword against nations, neither shall they learn war any more.

B. Christ and the Majesty in His Name - Isaiah 9:6...For unto us a child is born, unto us a son is given: and the government shall be upon his shoulder: and his name shall be called Wonderful, Counselor, The might God, The everlasting Father, The Prince of Peace.

C. Christ and a Victory That is Never Ending - 1 Thessalonians 4:17...Then we which are alive and remain, shall be caught up together with them in the clouds to meet the Lord in the air: and so shall we ever be with the Lord. Revelation 19:11-16...behold a white horse; and he that sat upon him was called Faithful and True, and in righteousness he doth judge and make war, verse 14...and the armies which were in heaven followed him, verse 15...And out of his mouth goeth a sharp sword. Revelation 19:21... And the remnants were slain with the sword of him that sat upon the horse, which sword proceeded out of his mouth. Revelation 21:1-2...And I saw a new heaven and a new earth, verse 2...And I John saw the holy city, new Jerusalem coming down from God out of heaven, prepared as a bride adorned for her husband.

II. Principals of Peace - 1 Samuel 17:10, 26, 45-47... And the Philistine said, I defy the armies of Israel this day give me a man, that we may fight together. Verse 26...And David spake o the men...who is this uncircumcised Philistine, that he should defy the armies of the living God? Verses 45-47... Then said David to the Philistine, Thou comest to me with a spear, and with a shield: but I come to thee in the name of the Lord of hosts, verse 46...This day will the Lord deliver thee into mine hand, verse 47...And all this assembly shall know that the Lord saveth not with sword and spear: for the battle is the Lord's...

III. People of Peace - Romans 12: 18-19... If it be possible, as much as lieth in you, live peaceably with all people, verse 19...avenge not yourself, but rather give place unto wrath: for it is written Vengeance is mine; I will repay saith the Lord. Psalm 34:14...Depart from evil, and do good; seek peace, and pursue it.

Chapter 17 - Religious Liberty

God alone is Lord of the conscience, and He has left it free from the doctrines and commandments of men, which are contrary to His Word or not contained in it. Church and state should be separate. The state owes to every church protection and full freedom in the pursuit of its spiritual ends. In providing for such freedom, no ecclesiastical group or denomination should be favored by the state more than others. Civil government being ordained of God, it is the duty of Christians to render loyal obedience thereto in all things not contrary to the revealed will of God. The church should not resort to the civil power to carry on its work. The gospel of Christ contemplates spiritual means alone for the pursuit of its ends. The state has no right to impose penalties for religious opinions of any kind. The state has no right to impose taxes for the support of any form of religion. A free church in a free state is the Christian ideal, and this implies the right of free and unhindered access to God on the part of all men, and the right to form and propagate opinions in the sphere of religion without interference by the civil power.

Genesis 1:27; 2:7; Matthew 6:6-7,24; 16:26; 22:21; John 8:36; Acts 4:19-20; Romans 6:1-2; 13:1-7; Galatians 5:1,13; Philippians 3:20; 1 Timothy 2:1-2; James 4:12; 1 Peter 2:12-17; 3:11-17; 4:12-19.

I. Christian Liberties Protected From the State - Amendment I of the United States Constitution...Congress shall make no laws respecting an establishment of religion or prohibiting the free exercise thereof.

    A. Freedom to Choose - religion/denomination

    B. Freedom to Congregate - time/place/manner

    C. Freedom to Communicate - teach/preach/message

    D. Freedom to Challenge - Constitutionally to preserve our rights

II. Citizen Responsibilities Prescribed By the Savior

    A. Prayer for those In Authority - 1 Timothy 2:1-3...first of all, supplications, prayers, intercessions, and giving of thanks, be made for all men, verse 2...For kings, and for all that are in authority that we may lead a quiet and peaceable life in all godliness and honesty...verse 3...For this is good and acceptable in the sight of God our Savior.

    B. Policy toward those Exercising Authority - Luke 20:22-25... Is it lawful for us to give tribute to Caesar, or no?...verse 24...shew me a penny. Whose image and superscription hath it? They answered Caesar's, verse 25...And he said unto them, Render therefore unto Caesar the things which be Caesar's, and unto God the things which be God's.

    C. Priority regarding Relationships with those in Authority - Acts 4:19-20...and said unto them, Whether it be right in the sight of God to hearken unto you more than unto God, judge ye...For we cannot but speak the things which we have seen and heard. 2 Corinthians 6:14...Be ye not unequally yoked together with unbelievers: for what fellowship hath righteousness with unrighteousness and what communion hath light with darkness? Romans 12:2...And be not conformed to this world: but

be ye transformed by the renewing of your mind, that
ye may prove what is that good, and acceptable, and
perfect, will of God.

Chapter 18 - The Family

God has ordained the family as the foundational institution of human society. It is composed of persons related to one another by marriage, blood, or adoption.

Marriage is the uniting of one man and one woman in covenant commitment for a lifetime. It is God's unique gift to reveal the union between Christ and His church and to provide for the man and the woman in marriage the framework for intimate companionship, the channel of sexual expression according to biblical standards, and the means for procreation of the human race.

The husband and wife are of equal worth before God, since both are created in God's image. The marriage relationship models the way God relates to His people. A husband is to love his wife as Christ loved the church. He has the God-given responsibility to provide for, to protect, and to lead his family. A wife is to submit herself graciously to the servant leadership of her husband even as the church willingly submits to the headship of Christ. She, being in the image of God as is her husband and thus equal to him, has the God-given responsibility to respect her husband and to serve as his helper in managing the household and nurturing the next generation.

Children, from the moment of conception, are a blessing and heritage from the Lord. Parents are to demonstrate to their children God's pattern for marriage. Parents are to teach their children spiritual and moral values and to lead them, through consistent lifestyle example *and loving discipline, to make choices based on biblical truth. Children are to honor and obey their parents.*

Genesis 1:26-28; 2:15-25; 3:1-20; Exodus 20:12; Deuteronomy 6:4-9; Joshua 24:15; 1 Samuel 1:26-28; Psalms 51:5; 78:1-8; 127; 128; 139:13-16; Proverbs 1:8; 5:15-20; 6:20-22; 12:4; 13:24; 14:1; 17:6; 18:22; 22:6,15; 23:13-14; 24:3; 29:15,17; 31:10-31; Ecclesiastes 4:9-12; 9:9; Malachi 2:14-16; Matthew 5:31-32; 18:2-5; 19:3-9; Mark 10:6-12; Romans 1:18-32; 1 Corinthians 7:1-16; Ephesians 5:21-33; 6:1-4; Colossians 3:18-21; 1 Timothy 5:8,14; 2 Timothy 1:3-5; Titus 2:3-5; Hebrews 13:4; 1 Peter 3:1-7.

The First Not Good in the Bible, Genesis 2:18...And the Lord God said, It is not good that the man should be alone.

I. Establishing the Institution of Marriage

    A. Literally Begins as a <u>Part</u>nership - Genesis 2:21-22...And the Lord God caused a deep sleep to fall upon Adam,... and he <u>took one of his ribs</u>, verse 22...and <u>the rib</u>, which <u>God had taken from man</u>, made he a woman...

    B. Realistically Begets Permanence
        1. Leaving - From...Genesis 2:24...leave his father and mother
        2. Cleaving - To...Genesis 2:24...cleave unto his wife
        3. Weaving - Form...Genesis 2:24...they shall be one flesh
        4. Achieving - Timeless...Matthew 19:6...what therefore *God hath joined together,* let not man put asunder

II. Ensuring the Integrity of the Family

    A. The Wife's Loving Spirit Toward Her Husband
        1. Submissive to her husband's authority...Ephesians 5:22...Wives, submit yourselves unto your own husbands, as unto the Lord, Colossians 3:18...as it is fit in the Lord

2. Subjection to her husband's authority...Ephesians 5:24...Therefore, as the church is subject unto Christ, so let the wives be to their own husbands in everything. If a woman's submission/subjection to her husband is implicit, then her selection of her husband is imperative. **As a wife is to submit to her husband's Authority... The husband...**

B. The Husband's Loving Service To His Wife

    1. Sacrificially for the needs of his wife Ephesians 5:25... Husbands, love your wives even as Christ also loved the church and gave himself for it. Husbands are to give...

        a. For her Provision-Physically For her

        b. Protection-Emotionally as Christ did sacrificially for the church...Ephesians 5:25

    2. Specifically for the nobility of his wife

        a. For her Preparation-Spiritually

        b. For her Presentation-Lovingly as Christ did to sanctify the church, Ephesians 5:26-27 ...the husband is not to be Authoritative as he leads his wife.

C. The Husband and Wife's Loving Strategy for Their Children

    1. Spiritual training

        a. Proverbs to Live By...Proverbs 22:6...Train up a child in the way he should go: and when he is old, he will no depart from it.

        b. Principals to Love By...Ephesians 6:4... ye fathers, provoke not your children to wrath: but bring them up in the nurture and admonition of the Lord

        c. Punishment to Learn By...Proverbs 13:24... He that spareth his rod hateh his son:...

            i. Not to condone abusive corporeal punishment... but: he that loveth him chasteneth him early

            ii. but to correct offensive character peculiarities

2. Solemn treatment - teaching them to be responsible, training them to be respectful.

   Remember: These are <u>Biblical Principles</u> for spiritual training, <u>not necessarily Biblical Promises</u> of spiritual training as children have to bring themselves under the authority of God through salvation

D. The Children's Loving Situation With Their Parents
   1. Special obligation...to parents....Proverbs 4:1... Hear, ye children, the instruction of a father, and attend to know understanding, Proverbs 13:1...A wise son heareth his father's instruction. Colossians 3:20...Children, Obey your parents in all things. Ephesians 6:2...Honor thy father and mother.
   2. Spectacular satisfaction...from God...Colossians 3:20...children obey your parents in all things for this is well pleasing unto the Lord.

Endnote

In the final editing phase for this book, my editor suggested we needed to add a few pages. After giving it some thought, I understood there was something fundamentally missing from the words I had penned – my testimony. As such, I realized, and am actually embarrassed to admit, I would be remiss in not sharing the circumstances leading to my accepting Christ as my personal savior. Salvation is a miracle and I experienced such a miracle. You have probably heard testimonies of those who Christ saved from a life of alcohol or drug abuse. Or maybe you know someone who was on the brink of fiscal collapse or was the victim or instigator of a dysfunctional personal relationship resulting in his or her coming to Christ.

My testimony is none of the above. In fact, I believe it to be more compelling, as by all accounts, I did not need a savior. For the most part as a child, I was obedient and compliant. Through my younger and mid teen years during the 60s and 70s, I did not consume alcohol, take illicit and mind altering drugs, nor was I sexually active, which for that time, made me a bit abnormal. Actually, my attitude was counter cultural as I did not "do it" because "everyone else was doing it," a popular theme of the times. So in that regard, I was a rebel. Bottom line, a person who has experienced the fruit of their sin understands their need to change their lives, but that was not my plight.

In high school, athletics makes for popularity and prestige. As an athlete, I had both and one of those perks lead to me my election as vice president of our high school's chapter of the Fellowship of Christian Athletes (FCA). I had attended meetings, but even now cannot remember what we discussed, except for one meeting in which I played and contrasted the words of a popular song of the times to the greatness of God. I hope that it did not damage the cause of Christ. As my family never attended church, God was more conceptual than personal. I understood right from wrong and presumed if one picked right, they picked God's side; pick wrong, the devil's side. Evaluating my spiritual life at the time, I was looking pretty good.

As a FCA officer, I had the opportunity to attend its camp in Rome, Georgia. The weeklong camp revolved around morning teaching sessions, athletic competition, and then nightly assemblies led by famous professional and college athletes, all spiritually based. A minister-humorist, Grady Nutt conducted all the morning sessions. He used his book, *Being Me-Self, You Bug Me* which revolved around the statement, "I am a person of worth, created in the image of God, to relate and to live" as the theme for each session. Using that statement and his wit and practicality, he helped me realize that God, through the revelation of His Son Jesus Christ, was more than a spiritual concept and that I could be involved with Him in a personal relationship. Because of his teachings, by my bedside after a night session, I asked Jesus to forgive me of my sin and to be my Lord and Savior. Without realizing it, I had gone from convicted sinner to converted Christian.

Returning home, I went as a new, yet baby Christian. As mentioned previously, my family did not go to church and unfortunately, I remained in an infant state spiritually. My family neither condoned nor condemned my newfound Christianity, but did not do anything to facilitate it. I knew if I were to die, my destination was heaven, but there was still the here and now I needed to deal with. It was not until graduating from high school and my first car that I began a spiritual growth spurt. With my new transportation, I was able to drive myself to church. In fact, when a young lady asked me to go to church with her my response was that I knew all about that "stuff." At that point, I really did not know what I did not know. I also made a public profession of my faith in that church when I followed the Lord in Believers' Baptism.

By God's grace and the miracle of my salvation in the summer of 1971, He has continued to teach me. Some lessons I learned faster, others slower, but my spiritual education has continued. However, I can and do say with all conviction I took learning the Word and Ways of God very seriously. I knew it was my responsibility to take advantage of solid Biblical doctrine and to know in whom and what I believed. God has graciously allowed me to share what He has taught me to others along the way, which is probably why he taught it to me. This book is an outgrowth of the Grace He has shown me and if He so wills, others will share in His Amazing Grace, grow, and share it with others as a result; however, our first responsibility is to know what we believe. May this book help facilitate that process.

Scripture Index

By Chapter and Page Number

Genesis

1:1	2, 5, 6, 39
1:2	5, 12
1:26-30	15
1:26	5, 16
1:26-28	72
1:27	67
2:5,7,18-22	15
2:7	6,16
2:15-25	72
2:17	16
2:21-22	72
2:24	72
3	15
3:1-20	72
3:5	16
3:6	16
3:8	16
3:8-11	20
3:15	5,20
3:21	20
9:6	15
12:1-2	7
12:1-3	25,45
12:21	54
14:20	53
14:22	54
15:1-5	54
17:1	6
18:1ff	8
20:3-17	61
22:8	20

Exodus

3:14	6
3:14-17	20
4:22	2
6:2,3	6
6:2-8	20
12:5-13	20
12:11-12	58
12:13	58
12:14	21
13:19	58
15:11ff	6
16:12	7
17:7	7
17:12	57
18:17ff	57
19:5-6	45
19:5-8	25
20:1ff	6
20:8	35
20:8-11	35
20:9-11	35
20:10	36,72
20:11	35
24:4	1

Leviticus

6:2-5	61
22:2	6
27:30	54
27:30-32	53
27:31-32	54
27:32	54

Numbers

15:30	17

Deuteronomy

8:18	53
4:1-2	1
4:1,5,9,14	49
6:1-10	49
6:4	6
6:4-9	72
10:12	61
17:19	1

27:17	61
31:12-13	49
32:6	6

Joshua

1:8	3
6:3	58
6:20	58
8:34	1
24:15	72
24:32	58

Judges

7:21	57
14:6	12
24:15	72

1 Samuel

1:26-28	72
8:4-7,19-22	25
17:10,26,45-47	66

2 Kings

6:6	4

1 Chronicles

21:1	18
29:10	6

Ezra

1:3-4	57
2:68-69	57
5:14-15	57

Nehemiah

2:3,6,8	50
4	57
8:1-5	57
8:1-8	49
8:3	50
8:2,5	50
8:5-6	50

Job

1:6-12	18
26:13	12
28:28	49

Psalms

1	15
2:7ff	8
8:3-6	15
8:4-6	26
19:1-3	6
19:1	3
19:1-6	2
19:7	3
19:7ff	49
19:7-10	1
19:13	17
19:14	21
32:1-5	15
34:14	66
51:4	16
51:5	15,72
51:11	12
78:1-8	72
101:5	61
110:1	9
110:1ff	8
119:1-176	3

119:11	49
119;11,89,105,140	1
119:41	23
119:133	17
122:1	29
127	72
128	72
139:7ff	12
139:8-10	7
139:13-16	72
147:4	6

Proverbs

1:8	72
3:13ff	49
4:1	74
4:1-10	49
5:15-20	72
6:20-22	72
8:1-7,11	49
12:4	72
13:1	74
13:24	72,73
14:1	72
15:14	49
17:6	72
18:22	72
22:6	73
22:6,15	72
23:13-14	72
24:3	72
29:15,17	72
31:10-31	72
96:9	35

Ecclesiastes

4:9-12	72
7:19	49
9:9	72

Isaiah

1:2	2
2:4	43,65
5:1-7	25
6:1-8	45
6:5	15
6:8	47
7:13	9
7:14	8,9
9:6	9,65
9:6-7	39
11:9	43
14:12-17	18
34:16	1
40:8	1
43:3	6
43:15	6
53	8
53:7	46
61:1-3	12
64:8	6

Jeremiah

1:4	2
10:10	6
14:13-17	16
15:16	1
17:5	15
17:15	6
23:5-6	39
30:2	2
31:31ff	25
36:1-32	1

Ezekiel

3:12	13
3:18	47
28:12-15	18

Daniel

4:8-9	13

Joel

2:28-32	12

Jonah

6:8	61,62

Zechariah

8:16	61,62

Malachi

2:14-16	72
3:10	55
3:11	55
3:7-12	54
3:8-12	53

Matthew

1:6	11
1:18	9,12
1:18-23	8
1:19	10
1:20-25	10
1:21	9,20
2:1,9	9
2:4	11
3:2	39
3:13-15	31
3:13-17	31
3:15	32
3:16	5,12,32
3:17	5,8
4:1	12
4:1-11	9
4:8-9	36
4:8-10,23	39
4:9-10	36
4:17	20
4:23	50
5:2	49,50
5:9,38-48	65
5:13	62
5:13-16,43-48	61
5:14,16	62
5:17-18	1
5:31-32	72
6:1-4,19-21	53
6:6-7,24	67
6:9ff	6
6:13	41
6:15-16,18	36
6:33	36,65
7:11	6
7:24ff	49
8:29	8
9:37-38	45,47
10:5-15	45,57
10:29-30	7
11:27	8
12:1-2	36
12:1-12	35
12:8	36
12:9	36
12:25-28	39
12:28-32	12
13:1-52	39
13:18-30,37-43	45

13:24-25	40	23:23	53	12:41-44	55
13:30	40	24:14	45	14:22-26	31
13:31-32	40	24:22,31	25	16:1-7	35
13:33	40	24:27,30,36,44	43	16:15	46
13:44	40	25:14-29	53		
13:45	40	25:31-46	39,43	**Luke**	
13:46	41	25:34	25		
13:47	41	25:35	61	1:27	10
13:49	41	26:29	39	1:28	10
13:52	41	26:26-30	31	1:32	9
14:33	8	26:52	65	1:34	10
16:15-19	27	26:64	43	1:35	8,12
16:16,27	8	27	8	1:42	10
16:18	28,37	27:51	28	1:68-69	20
16:18-19	25	28:1ff	35	1:68-79	25
16:19	45	28:1-6,19	8	2:11	9
16:21-26	20	28:18	45	2:20-25	68
16:26	15,40,67	28:18-20	45	2:28-32	20
16:27	43	28:19	5,6,12	2:29-32	25
17:5	8	28:19-20		2:40	49
18:2-5	72		31,46,49,57	2:46-47	50
18:8-9	43	28:20	46	3:21-22	31
18:15-17	63			4:1,18-19	12
18:15-20	27	**Mark**		4:18-21	61
18:17	26			4:41	8
19:3-6	72	1:1	8	4:43	39
19:6	72	1:9-11	6,31	4:43-44	41
19:21	53	1:14-15	39,41	6:27-28	63
19:28	43	1:10,12	12	6:38	62
20:1-6	57	1:29-34	61	8:1	39,50
20:28	21	2:3	57	9:2	39
21:28-45	25	2:3ff	61	10:1ff	57
22:1-10	57	2:27-28	35	10:1-18	45
22:9-10	45	2:38	50	10:2	47
22:17,21	63	3:11	8	10:18	18
22:21	67	8:38	43	10:27-37	61
22:29	1	9:1	39	10:33-37	62
22:36-40	61	9:43-48	43	11:13	12
22:37	62	10:6-12	72	11:41-42	55
22:39	62	10:21	61	11:42	55
23:9	6	10:45	21	12:12	12

12:16-21,42	53	4:24	6,12	20:21	45
12:31-32	39	5:24	20,25	20:25	17
12:40,48	43	5:26	6		
16:1-13	53	5:39	1	**Acts**	
16:19-26	43	6:44-45,65	25		
17:20-21	39	8:16	21	1:6-7	39
17:22-37	43	8:36	67	1:7	6
19:10	9,46,50	8:58	9	1:8	12,45,46
19:41-44	25	10:9,28-29	20	1:9	8
20:25	61	10:17-18	21	1:9-11	44
21:27	44	10:27-29	25	1:11	43
21:27-28	43	10:30,38	8	1:13-14	57
21:33	1	11:25-27	8	2	45
22:19-20	31,33	12:44-50	8	2:1-4,38	12
22:70	8	14:1-3	43	2:1ff	57
23:42	39	14:6	12	2:16ff	1
23:43	32	14:6-13	6	2:4,8	14
24:1-3,33-36	35	14:7-11	8	2:14,41	58
24:44-46	1	14:9-11	9	2:21	20,32
24:46-53	45	14:11-12	45	2:22-24	8
24:46	8	14:16-17,26	12	2:38,42,46	37
24:44-48	25	14:17	13	2:41-42	31
24:49	12	15:1-16	20	2:41-42,47	27
		15:7-8,16	45	2:41-42,44,46-47	28
John		15:12	61	2:44-47	53
		15:16	25	3:3	22
		15:26	12	3:5	22
1:1	2	16:7	12	4:12	20
1:12-14	25	16:7-14	12	4:19-20	67,68
1:11-14,29	20	16:13-15	1	4:29,31	46
1:14	5	16:15-16,28	8	4:31	12,47
1:18,29	8	17:1-5,21-22	8	4:31-37	57
1:29	21,46	17:1-8	6	5:1-11	53
3	11	17:3	7	5:3	12
3:3	39,41	17:6,12,17-18	25	5:11-14	27
3:16	25	17:15	45,61	6:1-2	29
3:16-17	3,40	17:17	1,20	6:3	12
3:16,18	32	18:16	39	6:3-6	27
3:3-21,36	20	19:33	9	6:8	29
3:23	31	20:1,19-28	35	7:55	12
4:3	44	20:1-20,28	8	7:55-56	8
4:21-24	35				

8:12	32	**Romans**		7:19	17	
8:17,39	12			8:1-18,29-39	20	
8:26	13	1:3-4	8	8:1-3,34	8	
8:26-40	45	1:7	27	8:14-15	6	
8:29	12	1:16	47	8:14-18,29	15	
8:29,35,38	58	1:16-18	20	8:16	12	
8:35-39	31	1:17	23	8:16-17	26	
8:36-37	32	1:18-32	72	8:18	22	
9:4-5,20	8	1:19-20	3	8:19	39	
10:42-48	45	1:19-32	15	8:35,35,37-39	26	
10:44	12	1:20	3	10:4	8	
13:1-3	27	1:28-31	17	10:9-10,13	20	
13:2	12	2:4	20	10:13-15	45	
13:2-3	45,57	3:10	46	10:17	22	
14:17	2	3:10-18,23	15	12:1-2	53	
14:23,27	27	3:23	17,46	12:2	68	
15:1-30	27	3:23-25	20	12-14	61	
15:1-35	57	3:23-26	8	12:4-6	58	
15:11	20	3:25	21	12:18-19	65,66	
15:28	12	3:26	26	13:1-7	65,67	
16:5	27	3:28	22	13:11-14	20	
16:6	12	3:29-30	22	14:5-10	35	
16:7	12	4:3ff	20	14:10	43	
16:30-31	20	4:4-5	26	14:19	65	
16:30-33	31	4:5	23	15:4	1	
17:11	1	5:1	25	16:25-26	1	
17:22-31	39	5:6,12,19	15			
17:24-25	53	5:6-21	8	**1 Corinthians**		
17:26-31	15	5:8-10	20			
17:30-31	20	5:12,18	17	1:1-2	25	
17:31	43	5:17	39	1:2	27	
19:1-6	12	6:1-2	67	1:10	59	
20:7	31,35	6:1-5	32	1:12-13	59	
20:28	27	6:1-23	20	1:10-17	57	
20:32	20	6:3-5	31	1:18,30	20	
20:35	53	6:6	15,22	1:18-31	49	
		6:6-22	53	1:21-31	15	
		7:14-25	15	1:30	8	
		7:15	16	2:2	8	
		7:15-20	2	2:10-11	13	
		7:18	17	3:6	58	

3:16	27	8-9	53,57	4:6	6
3:5-15	57	8:9	8	4:7-10	8
4:1-2	53	9:7	55	4:11-16	20,49
4:5	43	12:15	53	4:17-18	17
5:4-5	27			4:24-29	46
5:9-10	61	**Galatians**		4:30	13
6:1-7	61			5:1	46
6:19	13	1:6-10	57	5:18	14
6:19-20	20,53	2:11-14	59	5:21-33	72
7:1-16	72	2:16	26	5:22	72
7:17	27	2:20	20	5:22-32	27
7:20-24	61	3:13	20	5:24	73
8:6	6,8	3:26,29	28	5:25	41,73
9:13-14	27	3:26-28	61	5:26-27	73
10:16-17	33	4:4-5	8	6:1-4	72
10:16,21	31	4:6	6	6:2	74
10:23-11:1	61	5:1,13	67	6:4	73
11:23-29	31	5:22-23	14	6:5-9	61
11:26	33	5:23-25	20		
11:28	33	6:15	20	**Philippians**	
12	27,53,57				
12:7,28	14			1:1	27
15:1-8,24-28	8	**Ephesians**		1:15-18	57
15:24-28	25,39			2:5	59
15:10	20	1:4-23	25	2:5-11	8
15:19,21-22	15	1:7	20,21	2:12-13	20
15:24-28,35-58	43	1:13	13	3:15	59
15:52	44	1:20	8	3:20	67
15:52-57	44	1:22-23	27	3:20-21	43
16:1-2	35	2:1-10	25	4:8	49
16:1-4	53	2:1-22	15	4:10-19	53
		2:2	18		
2 Corinthians		2:8	23,26	**Colossians**	
		2:8-22	20		
5:10	43	2:9	26	1:5	6,43
5:17	22	2:19-22	27	1:9-22	20
5:17-20	20	2:20	41	1:12-14	25
5:19-21	8	3:1-11	25,45	1:13	39
5:21	21	3:8-11,21	27	1:13-22	8
6:14	68	3:11	8	1:14	21
6:17	46	4:1-16	57	1:18	27

1:21-22	15
2:3,8-9	49
2:9	8,9
2:10	9
2:12	31
2:16	35
3:1ff	20
3:4	43
3:9-11	15
3:12-17	61
3:16	35
3:18	72
3:18-21	72
3:20	74

1 Thessalonians

1:8	45,47
3:12	61
4:14-18	8,43
4:16-17	3,44
4:17	44,66
5:1ff	43
5:23-24	20

2 Thessalonians

1:7ff	43
1:13	7
2	43
2:13-14	25

1 Timothy

1:3-7	49
1:17	6
2:1-2	67
2:1-3	68
2:5-6	8
2:9-14	27

3:1	29
3:1-15	27
3:2-7	29
3:8-13	29
4:1	13
4:2	17
4:14	27
5:8,14	72
6:14	43

2 Timothy

1:3-5	72
1:12	20,25
2:10,19	25
2:15	49
3:14-17	49
3:15-17	1
3:16	2,8
3:16-17	3
4:1	29
4:1,8	43
4:5	45
4:8	43

Titus

2:3-5	72
2:13	43
2:11-14	20
2:13	43
2:13-14	8

Philemon

1	61

Hebrews

1:1-2	1
1:1-3	8
2:1	48
2:1-3	20,45
4:12	1
4:14-15	8
4:16	28
5:8-9	20
5:12-6:3	49
7:14-28	8
9:12-15,24-28	8
9:24-28	20
9:27-28	43
10:19	28
10:23	29
10:25	29
11:1	22
11:1-12:8,14	20
11:6	6,23
11:10,16	39
11:39-40	27
11:39-12:2	25,45
12:2	8
12:9	6
12:14	65
12:28	39
13:4	72
13:8	8

James

1:12	25
1:27	61
2:8	61
2:14-26	20
4:1-2	65
4:12	67
4:17	17
5:8	43

1 Peter

1:2-5,13	25
1:2-23	20
1:9	23
1:17	6
1:18-19	53
1:19	21
1:25	1
2:4-10	25,39,45
2:5	29
2:5,9,10	28
2:12-17	67
2:21-25	8
3:1-7	72
3:11-17	67
3:18	22,46
3:22	8
4:12-19	67
4:13	39
5:1-4	27

2 Peter

1:19-21	1
1:20-21	2
3:7ff	43
3:9	7

I John

1:6-2:11	20
1:7-9	8,25
1:18	17
2:2	21
2:19	25
2:20	12
2:28	43
3:2	8,22,25,43
4:10	21

4:14-15	8
5:4	23
5:7	5,6
5:9	8

2 John

7-9	8

Jude

14	43

Revelation

1:1	3
1:3	4
1:6,9	39
1:10	35
1:13-16	8
1:18	43
2-3	27
3:11	43
3:20	20
5:9-14	8
5:10	39
11:15	39
12:10	18
12:10-11	8
13:8	8
19:6	6
19:11-16	66
19:16	8
19:21	66
20:1-22:13	43
20:10	18
21:1-22:5	20
21:1-2	66
21:2-3	27
21-22	39
22:17	45

www.ingramcontent.com/pod-product-compliance
Lightning Source LLC
Chambersburg PA
CBHW020509030426
42337CB00011B/308

9 781604 520774